ABOUT

MW00777051

Approximately eighty wrote a book to guide published in 1930, the book offered perspective and inspiration to a country amidst war and social unrest. Today, America faces comparable political, economic and social challenges—yet, I feel confident that my great-grandfather's fundamental principals continue to resonate with truth. Diligence, self-reliance, altruism--and most importantly—unity, remain the solution to a brighter youth and a better America. It is my great privilege to share with you in its original format, "Making the Most of Yourself" written by James E. West.

My great-grandfather, James E. West, was a man who, despite adversity, dedicated his life to cultivating the Boy Scouts of America. His courage and devotion to this cause indubitably helped shape the group into the great organization it is today. Given the pervasive sense of uncertainty and insecurity plaguing the country today, I firmly believe both America and Scouting need this book more than ever. My great-grandfather's indefatigable spirit has served as my model and source of inspiration throughout my life, beginning when my mother read these quips to me as bedtime stories. I hope these short, simple chapters provide you with the same level of faith, motivation and will to ceaselessly strive towards achievement. Most importantly, I hope these short, simple stories provide you with the strength to maintain pure ideals amidst obstacles; for when man strives to improve himself, he strives to improve his country.

Yours Truly,
Andrew D. West
Great Grandson - James E. West

FROM THE COVER
OF THE FIRST EDITION:

This book represents the aims and ideals of the Boy Scouts of America as expressed through inspiring messages by the man who, more than any other, has made this great organization what it is. The book will be treasured by every Scout. Its wide scope is well illustrated in some of the chapter titles— "Initiative," "Stick To It," "Aim High," "Citizens," "Hobbies," "Books," "Obedience," "Making Good," "It Can Be Done," "Concentration," "Think Fast." Together these chapters and the others in the book form a composite picture of what the Boy Scout movement means to every boy and a man who is a part of it.

In his Introduction to this book, Theodore Roosevelt, Jr., says: "To me, Dr. West personifies our American way of thinking and living, and, in this book. Glowing with inspiration and hope for youth, I find incorporated his unquenchable patriotic spirit. As long as America has such men as he, we can face the future with confidence, and my earnest wish is that all thoughtful, aspiring boys of Scout age, together with their leaders, especially, may sometime be privileged to read "Making the Most of Yourself."

JAMES E. WEST

"Always, before making important decisions that will affect the lives of boys in Scouting, or those not directly influenced by the Movement, my eyes are drawn irresistibly for guidance and inspiration to the McKensie statuette of the Boy Scout on my desk, because that heroic little bronze figure symbolizes to me the boy-hood, not only in America, but throughout the world, to whom, both by design and desire, I have dedicated the utmost of my ability." These words express simply and poignantly the life of Dr. James E. West, Chief Scout Executive, Editor of "Boy's Life," and author of "Making the Most of Yourself."

The life story of Dr. West can be adequately described by one word—inspiration. Left an orphan at six, and despite the handicap of being a cripple, James E. West, by ambition and ability, fought his way up to become one of the most respected and honored men in America today. Early in Dr. West's career with the Boy Scouts, Theodore Roosevelt said of him: "You are one of those disinterested and patriotic citizens to whom this country stands under a peculiar debt of gratitude." On Dr. West's thirtieth anniversary as Chief Scout Executive, Franklin D. Roosevelt said: "Your service to Scouting over the years emphasizes the effectiveness of the American way of providing equal opportunity to youth. You have, through your work, rendered your country great service."

JAMES E. WEST, LL.D.

The crippled orphan boy who as Chief Scout Executive and Editor
of *Boys' Life* became the inspiring leader of millions of Boy Scouts.

MAKING THE MOST OF YOURSELF

The Boy Scout Trail
to the
Greatest of all Adventures

By

JAMES E. WEST

Chief Scout Executive, Boy Scouts of America
Editor, *Boys' Life, the Boy Scouts Magazine*

With an Introduction by
THEODORE ROOSEVELT, Jr.

Making the Most of Yourself is not an official publication of the Boy Scouts of
America. This product is not endorsed or sponsored by The Boy Scouts of
America. Boy Scouts of America®, BSA®, and Be Prepared® are trademarks
or registered trademarks of the Boy Scouts of America. Used with permission.

Printed in the United States of America

ISBN 978-0-578-03888-9

INTRODUCTION *

By Theodore Roosevelt, Jr.

THE Boy Scouts are an institution so firmly imbedded in our national life that it is hard to remember they were not always here. There are a million members; one boy in every three who reached the age of twelve last year became a Scout. Yet thirty years ago the Boy Scouts of America was but one of a dozen boys' organizations, all weak, all fumbling, all uncertain of their future.

From then to now, one man has planned and directed the Scouts' amazing growth. When the first modest beginnings were made, James E. West was persuaded to act as secretary for six months. The chore he planned to finish so promptly became a great career.

This man who, three decades later, is still on the job as Chief Scout Executive has been physically handicapped most of his life; he uses a cane, sometimes crutches. This man who leads and inspires a million boys spent his boyhood in an orphanage.

* Under the title, "America's Chief Scout," originally published in *Christian Herald;* afterward reprinted in *The Readers' Digest,* and now, with additions, admirably serving to introduce Dr. West's latest book.

Jim's father died before he was born. Destitute, his mother became a seamstress. When Jimmy was six, she died. At that time he was healthy and straight.

After a while, at an orphanage in Washington, D. C., Jimmy began to limp. The authorities decided he was malingering—to avoid being treated like the other children. So he was whipped. But his leg got no better. Then it was discovered that he had a tubercular hip. For nearly two years he was in a hospital, much of the time painfully strapped flat on his back. Pronouncing him "incurable," the hospital told the orphanage to take him back. The orphanage refused. Finally the hospital sent him to the orphanage without notice, leaving him on the doorstep with a small bag that held his few belongings.

So lame he couldn't do the work assigned to boys, Jimmy was put with the girls and taught to sew. It was here that Mrs. Ellis Spear, a friend of his mother, found him. She invited him to her home to play with her children. She gave him a children's book that she had written. On his next visit she asked him his opinion of the story. It was the first time any one had given him a chance to express himself, had placed any importance upon what *he* thought. There were more visits, more chances to talk freely. He expanded like a plant opening to the sun.

Most of the orphanage children were apprenticed as soon as they were old enough. But no one would take crippled Jimmy West. Presently he was the oldest boy at the institution, and began to help the matron. He was even given a small salary.

There was a library at the orphanage, usually locked. Because he had benefited from reading, Jimmy West asked permission to have the library opened to all. The matron was afraid the books would be injured. But Jimmy offered to get the other children to help him cover the thousand books with brown paper. This done, he catalogued them. Most of the children were not interested in reading; he offered to pay them, from his own wages, a cent for each book read. When that offer didn't stir up interest, he got permission for readers to sit up an extra hour in the evening. That worked!

He was learning how to get results.

He asked permission to go to public school, instead of attending the casual orphanage classes. Next he asked that some of the other children might go to public school, too, and agreed to be responsible for their homework. At one time there were twenty-four orphans attending public school with him.

At sixteen he finished the eighth grade and wanted to go on to high school. The idea of an orphanage

cripple going to high school was unheard of. Be-
sides, how could he do high-school work without neg-
lecting his duties at the orphanage? But the boy
was developing indomitable persistence. Could he try
it for a month? Reluctantly, permission was given.

He made good that month, both at school and at
the orphanage. He graduated from high school at
nineteen. His leadership of the orphan children had
made him a good mixer. He was editor of the school
paper, manager of the football team, and school li-
brarian. That he could find time and energy for these
activities without neglecting his work seems a mir-
acle. But he even took on the duty of night watch-
man.

West, now looking for a job, applied at a bicycle
shop. The owner said he could not employ a cripple.
West countered that he would learn to ride a bi-
cycle if it would get him the job. Touched by his
courage, the shop owner agreed. Naturally, with
one leg almost useless, Jimmy was unmercifully bat-
tered and bruised by falls, but he learned quickly
and got the job.

Next, West determined to walk without crutches.
For weeks he could barely keep his balance without
grabbing something, but he made it.

All this time he was intent upon improving con-
ditions at the orphanage. Superintending the chil-
dren, he helped them paint the whole place. There

was a campaign against rats; a man who owned
weasels was brought in to help. Next he went before
the directors and exposed waste and incompetence.
He showed that the money spent on food for 180
children, aside from bread and milk, was less than
that for the 14 members of the staff. The board was
shocked, and conditions were rectified.

Through the Y.M.C.A., where he found secre-
tarial work, he learned of a chance to read law with
an attorney. When he felt he needed further instruc-
tion, he entered the National University law school.

A fire in the Y.M.C.A. burned out the wing
where night classes were held. The directors said
they could not rebuild, and ordered night school
closed. This, to West, meant shutting the door of
opportunity on many young fellows. He sought per-
mission to take over the job of reopening the school,
including raising funds. West went to instructors, to
contractors, to all concerned, and asked them to
donate part of their services—or at least take de-
ferred payments. His persuasiveness brought one
"yes" after another; in short order the school was
reopened with a larger enrolment than before the
fire.

At twenty-five Jim West passed his bar examina-
tions. He secured an appointment to the Board of
Pensions, largely, I believe, through the interest
of my father, who had come to know him and ad-

mire his energy. Later he was made assistant attorney in the Department of the Interior.

During the half-dozen years he served in these capacities he took on any number of other activities. He fought before Congress for a much-needed school appropriation for Washington. He acted as General Secretary of the Y.M.C.A. It was he, backed by the Washington Playground Association, who first took up the question of turning the city's public parks over to children. With the support of my father, it was his agitation which got Washington its first Children's Court.

Later when some good people, whom Jim had interested in organizing a conference for the care of dependent children, wanted father to head it up, Jim West called on him, and as a result my father assumed leadership of the First White House Conference for the Care of Dependent Children. A letter of appreciation written by my father to Jim West after that conference, will be found on page xiv.

In 1909, the same year in which this letter was written, the Boy Scout movement was gaining momentum in England. An American newspaper man, William D. Boyce, was guided through a London fog by an English lad who refused to accept a tip.

"I'm a Scout," the boy said. "We don't take tips for favors."

Boyce was impressed. Back in this country he undertook the financing of an American Scout organization. There were movements of similar nature already in the field. Dan Beard had organized the Sons of Daniel Boone. Ernest Thompson Seton had begun the Woodcraft Indians.

There were also many smaller groups, some with Scout troops using the English uniform and methods of procedure. All had to be brought, without hurt feelings or loss of enthusiasm, into the main body of American Scouts.

Such a task required leadership of a high order. James West was invited to become secretary. At first he said it was impossible; he could not afford to give up his law practice and he felt his work among Washington children should not be neglected, but finally he agreed to take temporary charge.

To keep the growing organization non-sectarian and free from racial prejudice was a herculean task. Influential religious groups wanted to take control. A southern group served notice that if Negroes were included they would pile their Scout uniforms in the court-house square and burn them.

By tact and patience such obstacles were overcome. American Scouting is to-day as democratic as Indian corn. Its membership is drawn from every race and creed that go to make up our country.

Practically everything that West did in those

early days had to be done with limited facilities—
much of it single-handed. One thing needed was a
Scout handbook. Working day and night, West got
the material ready and had 5,000 copies printed.
He marked them "proof" and sent 4,600 to persons
interested in boys' work, asking for suggested im-
provements. A committee considered all comments
and redrafted the book. More than 6,000,000
copies of the Scout Handbook have been sold to
date.

Last year I stood on a platform at the New York
World's Fair and faced a gathering of 63,000 Boy
Scouts. James E. West was standing beside me—
without crutches. I thought of his story, from the
days when he was an unwelcome cripple in an orphan
asylum, and of the great movement which he had
been so instrumental in molding. And, in apprecia-
tion of so great an achievement, singularly, yet an-
other letter is addressed to Dr. James E. West from
the White House, this time signed by President
Franklin D. Roosevelt.

You will find both letters included on facing
pages. Reading them together, it may be observed
that my father's letter is somewhat prophetic, for
nearly thirty-two years ago he said of Dr. West,
"You are one of those disinterested and patriotic
citizens to whom this country stands under a pecu-
liar debt of gratitude."

To my father's words I would add these: Dr. West has been one of my intimate friends for twenty years, or more; our friendship has been founded on working together for the same objectives. To me, he personifies America, personifies our American way of thinking and living, and, in this book, glowing with inspiration and hope for youth, I find incorporated his unquenchable patriotic spirit. As long as America has such men as he, we can face the future with confidence, and my earnest wish is that all thoughtful, aspiring boys of Scout age, together with their leaders, especially parents, may sometime be privileged to read *Making the Most of Yourself*.

January 31, 1909.

My dear Mr. West:

I am glad to have thanked Mulry and Butler; out there is one man to whom preeminently our thanks are due, and that is you.   Mulry and Butler did work without which the conference would have been a failure; but if it had not been for you there would have been no conference whatever.   I have always thought well of you, but I now feel that you are one of those disinterested and patriotic citizens to whom this country stands under a peculiar debt of gratitude.

With all good wishes, believe me,

Sincerely yours,

Theodore Roosevelt

Mr. James E. West,
    1343 Clifton Street, N.W.,
        Washington, D.C.

May 16, 1941

Dear Dr. West:

During these perilous times I am more conscious than
ever of the patriotism of our Boy Scouts and the strength of
their leadership. To you belongs much of the credit for the
effectiveness of Scouting in this country. I desire therefore
to take this means, on your birthday, and on your thirtieth
anniversary as Chief Scout Executive, at the ceremonies in
your honor at Hillcrest, The Children's Village, Washington,
where you got your start in life, to tell you how much we
appreciate your accomplishments in behalf of American boyhood.

Your service to Scouting over the years emphasizes
the effectiveness of the American way of providing equal oppor-
tunity to youth. You have, through your work, rendered your
country great service and the prayer on my heart and the prayer
of countless Scouts and Scouters, too, I am sure, is that you
may be spared many years to carry on your activities in this
most important field of all opportunity.

Very sincerely yours,

Franklin D Roosevelt

Dr. James E. West,
Chief Scout Executive,
Boy Scouts of America,
2 Park Avenue,
New York, N. Y.

FOREWORD

FROM my office window I look out upon a gigantic structure, the Empire State Building. I saw them demolish the old, world-famous hotel that used to stand on this site. I saw them lay the foundations of the new buiding. The men who planned the Empire State Building had to take into consideration the possibility of earthquake, the possibility of cyclone, the possibility and probability of frequent electrical storms. They had to take into consideration a certain percentage of dampness in the course of 365 days in the year, and sudden ranges in temperature. This building had to be erected to stand, to be serviceable, to be productive. The architects, the engineers, by careful calculation, worked out every detail, and their efforts were justified. Each winter the building is subjected to tremendous strain during severe storms. Actually, this building sways, extending as it does over one hundred stories into the air. But the foundations and structure are such that it stands the strain.

What a tremendous satisfaction it must be to the architects and the engineers that they laid the foundations of the building well and solidly! Magnificent buildings, though, however beautiful and durable, are not the most valuable possessions of our great country. We are one hundred and thirty-one million people; they are our greatest asset! Of these millions, some twenty-six million are boys and young men under the age of twenty-one. Those who are older are pretty well fixed in their habits. Their foundations are finished. If those who were the architects and engineers of their lives, who were responsible for their education and training, did not do a thorough job, there is not much that can be done now. But with this group under twenty-one we have a tremendous opportunity! Those of us who care about youth have the opportunity of helping them to lay the right sort of foundations for life.

I speak with confidence. It has been my happy privilege to maintain a personal correspondence with over six thousand young men who were active Scouts a few years ago, attending Troop meetings, going to Scout Camp, working for Merit Badges and advancement to Star, Life, or Eagle rank, and generally having as much fun and receiving as much benefit from Scouting and their associates in the Troop as boys are receiving to-day. But they are older now. They have grown up and gone on through high school and into college, shouldering more responsibilities, working harder and preparing themselves to go out into the world and take their places as

citizens well able to do their share in furthering the
principles and ideals of democracy and the fine social
equality that is the foundation of Americanism.

I began this correspondence and maintained it be-
cause I first of all had a very deep personal interest
in these boys, as I have in all Scouts. I wanted to
know, too, their ambitions, the goals toward which
they were striving in college and, after college, and
just how much their Scout training and early asso-
ciations were helping them toward achieving their
ambitions.

I knew that I would get back some fine letters. I
knew that many of these boys would attest to the
fact that Scouting had done much for them both in
building character and in training them as fine up-
standing American citizens. I was not disappointed.
Indeed, very much to the contrary, I was filled with
satisfaction and deep happiness, for with great
enthusiasm these boys agreed that Scouting had
been the most moving influence in their lives toward
character building, outside of their own homes.

Scouting carries on! Scouting is a lasting influ-
ence! Scouting ideals and experiences are not mere
memories but are proving to be solid life founda-
tions. Because I believe this wholeheartedly, I have
accepted the suggestion that a volume of my *Boys'
Life* editorials be published, the selection to consist
of those that emphasize that Scouting provides for

a boy a way of life all-inclusive—that it encompasses not just his leisure time but, by purposeful motivation, all his time, and that, when his life is organized on this basis, a boy is able to enjoy the richest experience of which he is capable.

I sincerely hope that, in more permanent form, these *Boys' Life* editorials may inspire yet other boys to participate in the greatest adventure of all, the adventure of making the most of one's self by devotedly following the Scout Trail.

At this time I wish to express my appreciation to the hundreds of Scouts and Scout Leaders all over the country who have so generously sent me records, out of their own experience, that have helped to make possible many of the true stories included in this volume. I wish to thank them, and my associates at the Home Office also, for their encouragement and for their loyal coöperation without which it would hardly have been possible to produce this book. I regard all of these who have served in this undertaking as my associate editors and I ask that they accept this statement as a sincere expression of my thanks.

JAMES E. WEST
Chief Scout Executive, Boy Scouts of America
Editor, *Boys' Life,* The Boy Scouts Magazine

CONTENTS

CONTENTS

ILLUSTRATIONS

YOURSELF

AMONG all your friends, no matter how many they may be, there is one who is constantly with you, who knows everything you do, even those things you hope other people will not find out. He is the fellow who sometimes shirks his lessons; who is not always as careful, maybe, about his health habits as he might be; who sometimes fails to be as helpful at home as you know he ought. He is yourself!

You choose your friends because they are the kind of fellows you like. They are for the most part people you respect. Try to make this fellow that you have to live with all the time, the kind of person in whom you can take some satisfaction. Make him a boy you can esteem. Such a boy will be in good physical shape. He will learn the facts about his physical condition and observe the simple rules of health that will help to make and keep him physically fit. He may not be a brilliant scholar—not all of us have abilities of that sort; but he will not handicap his teachers or himself by neglect of his studies. He will definitely make an effort to live up to a code of conduct such as the Scout Oath and Law. He will place special emphasis on helpfulness to others. He will do all this not as a difficult task, but cheerfully.

One way to accomplish this is to try to act like some one you admire. What person in your reading, or in history, or perhaps in public life to-day, or in your home community would you most like to resemble? Make a study of the things in his character that you admire, and try to develop these qualities in yourself. Ask yourself what he would do in this situation, or in that; if he had a chance to do something that was not quite square—if he shirked staying home to help his mother in order to go to the ball game. Whenever you are in doubt about something, think what he would do—then do it.

It will not always be easy to make yourself the kind of boy you want for a friend, but if you will make an earnest and consistent effort, in proportion to your effort and ability, you will find that you achieve success and satisfaction. Try to make yourself the kind of boy you can like and respect.

> *This above all: to thine own self be true,*
> *And it must follow, as the night the day,*
> *Thou canst not then be false to any man.*
> —SHAKESPEARE

INITIATIVE

INITIATIVE! Why does one boy get ahead and another stay in a rut? Often it is more a matter of initiative than capability. Nothing worth while was ever accomplished without it. It was some one's initiative that has given us every invention that has ever advanced mankind. Initiative was responsible for the discovery of this continent, and it was initiative that drove our forefathers to found our nation.

Initiative is the ability to act without being told what to do. It is more than mere originality. Plenty of people have original ideas, but it takes something more to put them through and make them work. It can not be learned out of a book. It is something a boy must develop for himself. The whole program of Scouting was devised to help develop this quality and the other qualities of character that go with it.

Initiative is based on knowledge, knowledge of what to do and how to do it. It is based on energy, physical health, enthusiasm. The boy with initiative often advances more rapidly than a more brilliant boy. The boy who sits around and waits for somebody to give him directions, the boy who does only what he is told to do and nothing more, is not going to advance very rapidly in his school work, nor is he going to make a brilliant success in later life. Every walk of life, every business, our national political parties, are crowded with men who do only what they are told to do. It is the man with energy, ambition, and initiative that leads the way. You can not follow another person's footsteps and reach your goal. You must mark out a trail for yourself. But you can learn from the experiences of others, and you can if you will earnestly go about it, develop qualities in yourself that help to lead you to success.

Begin right now in your own home. Show initiative in doing things around the house that need to be done, even though no one has told you to do them, or even, perhaps, expects you to. There are many repairs in a house, many tasks that any active boy can handle. In your school work don't confine yourself merely to what the teacher tells you to study, but try to get a sound fundamental knowledge of the subject involved. Education is an essential basis for initiative. Study conditions in your church, in your school, and in your community. When you have a sound knowledge of all the factors involved, perhaps you can, with the help of others, develop something of lasting benefit.

Photo by New York Times Studio

THE WILL TO WORK AND WIN

In 1928 Eagle Scout Paul Siple was selected to go with Admiral Byrd to the Antarctic where he served as a biologist and zoölogist. He was Chief Biologist of Byrd's second Antarctic Expedition (1933-35) and led the Marie Byrd Land Exploring Party. In 1939-41 he was Leader in charge of the West Base of the United States Government's Antarctic Expedition.

The records of our Boy Scouts show that it is entirely within the powers of even a young boy to initiate and develop things that are really worth while in community life. The ideal Boy Scout is one who not only knows how to take care of himself, stand on his own feet, and carry his share of the load in his own home and the community of which he is a part, but plus this has the initiative and the training to care about helping others. He gives abundant evidence of his capacity to care for other people. He seeks opportunities to be useful and helpful. He makes his personality felt so that all are impressed with his sincerity, initiative, and character.

With all the changes that are taking place in the world to-day, initiative is more needed than ever, to take advantage of changed conditions and new opportunities. As I have often said, it is not that opportunity makes the man, but it is the man who makes the opportunity, or rather who has the initiative to know what to do with the opportunity when it is presented to him. When unexpected difficulties come up, it is the man who has initiative who devises ways to overcome them, and has the courage to adopt new methods.

Every great leader has initiative. There is no advance without it. Don't worry if you make a mistake at first. Every one does. But learn your lesson from it, so that you will never make that particular mistake again. Don't be conceited or cocksure. Those qualities come from lack of knowledge and lack of preparation. Be sure you are right—then go ahead.

> *The merit of originality is not novelty; it is sincerity. The believing man is the original man; whatsoever he believes, he believes it for himself, not for another.*
>   —CARLYLE

COURAGE AND CONFIDENCE

COURAGE involves much more than the bravery of one short moment—the swift leap to a rescue, the sudden daring that averts approaching danger. Courage, true courage, is largely a matter of right habits and persistent effort. It is based on confidence, intelligent confidence developed from a sound knowledge of the facts involved, and a thorough training that enables us to make the best use of our own capabilities.

Theodore Roosevelt was an outstanding example of this. He never expressed an opinion until he had first thoroughly informed himself on the subject. Then, with characteristic courage, and with confidence founded on intelligently developed information, he "hit the line hard." "Nothing," he once told a group of boys, "can make good citizenship in men who haven't in them courage, hardihood, decency, sanity, the spirit of truth-telling and truth-seeking, the spirit that dares and endures." He had weak eyes all his life, yet he became a successful hunter, an omnivorous reader, and a keen naturalist. He had lost the hearing in one ear, but he mastered his handicap and taught himself to distinguish even the calls of birds. He was a sickly, ailing boy who was not expected to live to manhood, but he overcame his physical ailments and became the very embodiment of vigorous life and outdoor activity.

A striking example of courage based on confidence is that of a Life Scout who rescued from drowning two young women who had been seized with cramps and had gone down two hundred feet from shore. He brought first one girl to safety and then went back for the other. The second girl was unconscious and he worked over her for half an hour before he was able to restore her. The Scout said, when commended, that his action was not prompted so much by bravery as by necessity. In an editorial on the case, the Toledo *Blade* remarked: "That was an honest and candid confession. The Scout saw that a life-saving job had to be done. Having been prepared by training to meet the emergency, he did it quickly and efficiently. His modesty is commendable, but his work nevertheless was heroic."

This boy's splendid courage was based on his confidence in his training and his knowledge of life-saving methods. "Be Prepared!" The Scout Motto is a challenge to every boy to secure the right training and develop his own powers so that he is equipped with a knowledge of the right thing to do and the ability to do it.

Courage involves character. Every day of your lives you are called upon to show courage. Every day you are placed in some situation that definitely tests you. It requires courage to practice patiently in spite of discouragement until you have acquired proper form in swimming, life-saving, or some other activity. Almost every step of progress that you make will be in the face of difficulty and discouragement. But don't let it beat you! Always do what you are afraid to do. Only in this way can a boy acquire real confidence in his own powers, and the character, self-control, and grit that enable him to do the thing that is right because his judgment tells him it is right, and refrain from doing the thing that is wrong because he knows it is wrong. Mere daring without character is not especially worth while. There are gangsters and other contemptible types that possess this kind of bravery. The right sort of courage must involve right thinking and right training and a worth-while objective.

Few men are born with courage. But any man can make himself brave if he tries, and especially if he begins trying when he is a boy. Learn to bear disappointment cheerfully and to work hard for what you know is worth while. Try to develop a strong body, and to secure the kind of knowledge and training that will equip you for the work that you are to do. Remember that every day of your life tests your character, and learn to meet each situation bravely and with confidence.

A wise statesman once said: "You will never do anything in this world without courage. It is the greatest quality of mind, next to honor."

> *When moral courage feels that it is in the right, there is no personal daring of which it is incapable.*
>
> —LEIGH HUNT

EQUIPPED

THIS is a story about confidence, about skill, and the power that comes from them. I like to think of it as a story of a boy, yes, several boys, who were *equipped*.

It was spring in northern Ohio, and on a certain Saturday afternoon a group of about twenty boys, a few of whom were Scouts, started for the creek for the first swim of the season.

As they neared the creek they were strung out in a long line down through the meadow, undressing as they ran, each trying for the honor of being "first in." (This story shows also the wisdom of the safety rules that we teach in Scouting, for if this group had followed those rules, what happened afterwards would never have occurred.)

What did happen was this. The first boy in the line was undressed as he reached the bank of the creek, made a dive into the water, went down, and did not come up. The second boy in line saw him dive in, quickly finished undressing, and went in after him. The second boy did not come up.

The third boy in line saw the second boy dive

in, but knew nothing about the first. He called to those behind him, went in after the second boy, recovered the body, and brought it out. Then the Scouts in the group sent one of them for a doctor, and began to give artificial respiration.

After a few minutes an eyelid fluttered; there was a gasp for breath. The boy woke up, looked around, and immediately said, "Where is Kenny?" None of them knew anything about Kenny, and only after questioning learned that he was still in the creek.

Again the Scouts went into action. They organized a search and eventually found Kenny's body. The body was brought out and the Scouts began to work on him. They worked over Kenny, with no results, and after what the boys believed was twenty minutes they decided it was no use. One said, "He's cold." Another said, "He's stiff." And another said, "He's blue." And another said, "He's dead."

Just then a fourteen-year-old Patrol Leader came running up; asked what had happened. They told him Kenny was dead. There was no use working any more. But the Patrol Leader's reaction was immediate. "The *Handbook* says," he declared, "that we have to work over him, if necessary, two hours."

He organized the other Scouts and they worked in shifts. After what seemed to them to be a half hour more, there was a sign of life, and eventually Kenny woke up.

Two lives were saved because of the fact that in this group of boys were a few Scouts who were equipped from the standpoint of knowledge, equipped from the standpoint of skill, equipped from the standpoint of character. No man in the history of the world ever accomplished anything unless he was equipped with these things.

> *Try to put well in practice what you already know; and in so doing, you will, in good time, discover the hidden things which you now inquire about.*
>
> —REMBRANDT

HABIT

EVERY day of our lives we are forming habits. Some of them are desirable, some are undesirable. But good or bad, your habits represent—YOU! There is nothing more binding than a habit, and few things that are harder to break. Science tells us that every time we do anything, in our actual physical brain there is made a slight furrow. When we repeat that action, we deepen that furrow. Our actions tend to follow the furrow as water runs down hill, and so we form a habit.

If you do a thing once in a certain way, it will be easier to do the next time in that same way and easier still the next, until in time no effort is required at all, and indeed to do the opposite would be difficult. Everybody knows how automatic the things become that we do habitually. Try moving the furniture in your room and note how you stumble over it until you have become accustomed to the new location.

In the same way we form habits of mind—habits of study, habits of punctuality, habits of cheerfulness. It is all the more important that we try to form the right sort of mental habits because we ourselves are often unaware that we are developing them, and only wake up to the situation when the furrows in our brain are deeply formed and the habit has become fixed. If we have developed the right sort of habits, our actions follow automatically the furrow, and the results are worth while to ourselves and to others.

We have it within our power to determine at all times what type of habits we shall form. Every boy can say to himself, "I will be what I want to be." The great law underlying character formation and character building is simple and natural, and any boy may follow the scientific method. Your every action is accompanied by a thought, or brain process. To a great extent, your thoughts determine your actions. It is largely within a boy's own hands what thoughts he shall permit to remain in his mind. He can exercise a good deal of control over his mind; the effort to control his thoughts will result inevitably in influencing his actions. Each time the effort necessary to influence a particular action will become less, until the right sort of habit becomes fixed.

The best way to throw out an undesirable thought from your mind and to develop a good habit is to put in some worth-while thought instead. This may in time become the dominating thought and result in a definite course of action, which in turn may become a habit. In time a boy may acquire the habit of cheerfulness—or he may allow habit to make him irritable. Habit can make him punctual and orderly, or tardy and slovenly. It comes down to the matter of right thinking, and building correct habits.

> *A thought—good or evil—an act, in time a habit—so runs life's law: what you live in your thought-world, that, sooner or later, you will find objectified in your life.*
> —RALPH WALDO TRINE

THINK!

THE most important lesson that you can learn is one which is not taught in books—to *Think!* Education does not mean just knowing things. It means being able to *think for yourself*.

The most difficult thing for a boy to secure in education, I am told, is this ability to think for himself. It is so easy to follow and applaud. God forbid that schools in America should ever come to a point where they turn out graduates with their ideas all cut to a pattern, regimented, without a spark of individual initiative in the group.

Right now, what we need in our country is thinkers; we need men who are original and men whose minds have been trained on a democratic basis, the American Way.

Not only do I find great stimulation in reading good books, the daily press, current magazines, but in availing myself of the opportunity to hear men and women who are recognized as outstanding thinkers. Perhaps some of you may not agree with me, but I think it is very definitely my duty to plan to get two points of view. I am greatly stimulated, for instance, by reading a certain well-known national magazine. It is seldom that I can agree with what I read in that particular magazine, but nevertheless it is a stimulating thing to read it. I make it my business to read two newspapers. I commute, and can get en route to my office and en route home an opportunity to secure two extreme points of view editorially, and I like editorials. I have not very much sympathy with the policy of one of the newspapers, or the ideals for which the paper stands, but reading its editorials does give me an experience in thinking, and I recommend it. I recommend to you boys all processes which encourage and require thinking. After all, that is what your education is intended to do for you—to help you learn to think for yourself.

Never be discouraged or think that you are too young to form sound opinions. Some of the greatest contributions to science, economics, literature, and the world's progress have been made by young men, some of them scarcely older than many Scouts. Abraham Lincoln was only twenty-four when he first campaigned for public office. Newton was the same age when he formulated the law of gravitation. Stevenson wrote *Treasure Island* at thirty-three. Lindbergh flew the Atlantic when he was but twenty-five years of age. And so I might go on.

But remember, not one of these young men

achieved fame because he copied some one else's work. They intelligently informed themselves of the facts by a study of all the data available. Then— they were able to think for themselves, and learn. Above all—*think!*

> *Thinking, not growth, makes manhood.*
> *Accustom yourself, therefore, to thinking.*
> *Set yourself to understand whatever you*
> *see or read. To join thinking with reading*
> *is one of the first maxims, and one of the*
> *easiest operations.*
>
> —ISAAC TAYLOR

THINK FAST!

How fast can you think? In that split second when you have to decide to do one thing or another, can you make up your mind? Most outstanding people, you will find, think fast. Sometimes an entire baseball game hangs for a moment on one man's quick thinking. Sometimes it is a business opportunity that comes once in a lifetime. Sometimes a human life.

In a large Texas town a father was walking home from work. A little distance up the street he could see his home, and as he approached, the door burst open and the small figure of his baby son catapulted out of the house and tore down the street at top speed, arms wide spread, to meet his daddy. The baby started across the road just as a huge truck came rushing down upon him. No time for the father to reach the spot. Time only to shout a warning that fell on unhearing baby ears.

"Then," wrote the father later, "as though out of nowhere, out of an alley came a Scout." A split second to decide, with death roaring down the road. The Scout dashed forward. He caught the child to him and threw himself backward—no time even to turn around. To the father it looked as if both had gone under the wheels. But no, the Scout picked himself up, and soothing the crying child, handed him over to his father, walked down the alley, refused even to give his name. "It's nothing. I just had to think fast, that's all."

And a grateful father sat down and sent an account to the Scout office. "I'm only hoping that my boy will turn out to be a Scout some day," he wrote.

A story of courage, yes. A story of something besides courage—quick thinking. Another boy might have made that dash and, trying to turn, have gone under the wheels with the helpless victim. But this Scout could think fast.

The ability to think fast usually goes with good muscular coördination and an alert mind. You can in all probability develop these things if you try. Thinking fast often depends on the habit of thinking things through in advance. Perhaps our unknown Scout had planned what he would do, not just in an emergency like this one, but in other emergencies requiring quick thought and lightning-like action.

"Mentally awake!" We have that in our Scout Oath. Your happiness and your success depend to a large extent on your mental alertness. Can you think things through for yourself? Have you an enquiring mind? Is each day a new adventure for you because you learn something new, think out some new way of doing old things, move forward—never standing still?

The boy who is mentally awake lives more in a day than a dull boy does in a month. He has more adventure, he gets more out of life, and he gives more to other people. You want to have friends, of course you do. You want to excel in games, you want interesting hobbies. You have to bring interest to them. If you have a personality that is dull and uninteresting and unattractive, you will never get all that is coming to you out of life.

Learn to think fast! Think on your toes, poised for action.

> *Men must be decided on what they will not do, and then they are able to act with vigor in what they ought to do.*
>
> —MENCIUS

CONCENTRATION

SOME boys seem to accomplish as much in one hour as others do in two. They can finish their studies more quickly; they appear to have ample time for all sorts of worth-while interests, clubs, hobbies, athletics, church work, reading. Often this is not so much from their superior ability, but because they have learned how to hold their minds on what they are doing, and think of nothing else. This is called concentration, and it is one of the most important things a boy should learn, not only because it will make him more efficient, but because it will make it possible for him to do many more interesting things than he could otherwise have time for.

Keep a check on yourself and note how many times your mind wanders as you read this page. Some boys' minds fairly jump from one thing to another like an acrobat.

Mind wandering, wool gathering—how often we hear these expressions! Don't let your mind run away with you. Learn to command it. It is not easy, but it can be done.

Concentration is made up of will-power and

physical self-control. You can train your mind in much the same way as you train your body. Almost every boy knows that to be physically fit he must take exercise regularly. Otherwise his muscles will become soft and his body will not develop properly. In the same way, unless you work with concentration and push yourself constantly to do your best, your mind will not develop as it should, and when you get a hard job you will not be able to accomplish it quickly and effectively.

Train your mind so that it will do what you want it to do. Force yourself to keep your attention on the lesson or the job that you are doing. During an exciting football game you often become so absorbed in the play that you are practically unaware of everything around you except the ball and the players. No difficulty about concentration then. Bring that same intense quality to your work and see how much you can accomplish.

Notice how quickly you can do your homework if you can not go to the ball game until you have finished it. That proves that you can concentrate when you want to. Make yourself do the same thing every time you study. Give yourself a certain length of time to accomplish a definite amount of work. Then finish on time. Don't put off that job until you feel like doing it. Do it now! When you are a man, your work will not wait until you are in the

Photo by Roman Freulich

A VENTRILOQUIST MUST CONCENTRATE

Edgar Bergen, for five years a member of Troop I, Decatur, Michigan, learned to do that in Scout Troop and Camp. There, with Charlie McCarthy, at every opportunity, he perfected his developing skill. Mr. Bergen says, "I knew that with hours of practice I could improve my ability and, believe me, I practiced every chance I could."

mood to tackle it, and it is while you are young and in school that you should learn how to concentrate on it. Master your mind, don't be its slave!

Every boy should deliberately do something that is hard to do. Ask any man, old or young, what experience helped him most, and he will almost always tell you that it was the thing that made him work the hardest. It is the vigorous exercise that you need to train your mind. So don't pick out the easy courses in school, nor just the subjects you like the best. Choose at least one thing that will give you a real fight. Then beat it!

> *It is by hard work that man carves his way to that measure of power which will fit him for his destiny.*
>
> J. G. Holland

LOOK AND SEE

ONE afternoon, Bill, a Life Scout of a Troop in Baltimore, was sitting by a window in the living-room. Suddenly he saw a man in a greenish coat running down the avenue. He noticed that each hand was in a side pocket of the coat. Bill stiffened in his seat, his curiosity aroused. Why should a man run on this hot afternoon, and why should he keep his hands in his pockets?

Bill continued to watch him. At the corner the man stopped, looked around as though expecting some one, then turned back and ran into an alley across from Bill's home. Meanwhile, the man had taken his right hand out of his right pocket, but kept his left hand by his side, clutching something. He was small, dark, with regular features. Bill was rather specializing in observation and tracking, so he stayed by the window to watch. After a few moments the man came out of the alley and began to stroll toward the street corner again. Just then Bill heard the rumble of an automobile, southbound along the avenue. A large, dark green sedan with a woman at the wheel came swiftly past and slowed down.

Bill had been interested in automobiles—he wanted to qualify for the Automobile Merit Badge—and so he noted, and later was able to recall, the make and markings of the car.

At the corner the car slowed down but did not stop. While it was still in motion, the man hopped in and took the wheel while the woman moved over in the front seat. For a moment, while Bill watched, the man seemed to be talking furiously to the woman, then they drove off down the avenue and disappeared as they turned the corner.

A little later Bill was startled by the sound of sirens and shouts. A crowd was collecting and ran down the street, turning the corner where the car had disappeared. Bill decided to investigate. When he arrived on the scene, he found that a truck driver who had been making some large collections on bills had been held up. The police were on the scene, questioning him and others who had witnessed the hold-up. Their descriptions were very much confused. Bill started to tell some of his friends what he had observed when the police overheard him and began to ask him questions. His descriptions were so accurate and his memory so clear that within three days the arrest of a notorious criminal and his wife followed.

I have told you this story, not with the idea of encouraging you to qualify as junior detectives, but

to emphasize the importance of good observation
and an accurate memory. This incident illustrates,
furthermore, that it is within the capacity of boys
to develop these qualities, and that life will be very
much more of an adventure, very much more inter-
esting in all its routine activities, if you will take the
trouble to learn to make it so. That is one reason
why we, in the Scout Requirements, definitely made
tracking and observation a basis for advancement.
This enables a boy to take care of himself better in
the open and opens up a whole new field of interest
in life.

Try to cultivate your ability to notice things. Go
to camp and learn the habits of the wild life in the
woods around you. Learn to distinguish animal
tracks and bird calls and the different sounds in the
woods. Any boy can get observation experience on
hikes in the country. Practicing observation in the
city is something more of a test, but it is a habit
that can easily be acquired, as our friend Scout Bill
did.

Do not stop with merely the ability to observe.
You must learn to make deductions from what you
see. It is not enough just to look. You must see with
the eyes of the mind. If Bill had not known some-
thing about cars, he could not have furnished an ac-
curate description of the automobile. If his mind
had not been alert, he would never have noticed

that the man's actions were peculiar. As you observe more, you will want to learn more—learn more about the wild life in the woods, more about the clouds over your head, more about the people around you, yes, more about the community where you live and the laws that govern it, more about our democratic form of government and how we preserve it. A habit of observation can carry you on and on in ever-widening circles of interest. Look and see!

He is a great observer, and he looks
Quite through the deeds of men.
                    —SHAKESPEARE

GOALS

EVERY boy should determine for himself his goal in life. Can you imagine starting off for camp without knowing where you are going? Can you imagine two football teams beginning a game without finding out where the goal posts are? It is just as impossible to accomplish anything in life unless you have a definite understanding of what it is that you want to achieve.

Successful men will tell you that one of the most important goals for any boy is a life work in which he can take joy and satisfaction and which he can carry on effectively. This does not necessarily mean a job in which you will make a great deal of money. Some of the work that is richest in satisfaction does not bring very great returns in actual money.

Nearly every boy finds that it is hard to decide what he is going to be when he grows up, and that he needs help in making his choice. But there are certain things that you can do yourself to check on what line of work you are best fitted for. You can consider the things that you do most easily and most successfully—whether you are better at making model airplanes than at managing your school club, or in studying such things as languages and literature, for instance. The way in which you like to spend your leisure time is something of a guide, too. Make a list of the characters in history and fiction that you most admire. This will give a guide to your inclinations and character. Consult with your teacher, your Scout Leaders, and others who are in a position to know something about your abilities. See how nearly your tastes and talents measure up to the qualifications for the different professions.

In choosing your life work, remember that it is not so much what you get out of it as what you put into it that will give you satisfaction.

Another goal is a wide scope of interests. Try to cultivate hobbies. The man who knows only one thing in life and can do only one thing is apt to be bored. If you are a good swimmer, learn to be a good skater, too, so that you have a wholesome interest to carry you through the months when you can't swim. If you like to make model airplanes, learn something about radio. You will find that each new hobby makes life much more interesting for you. We in Scouting are trying to encourage boys to develop hobbies through the Merit Badge Program. But any boy can develop hobbies for himself.

Another goal should be friends and a happy home. If you have a warm and genuine interest in other people and want to be of service to them, you can't help attracting friends. The spirit of the Boy Scout Good Turn is the basis of friendship, and the boy who has acquired the Good Turn habit is sure to have hosts of friends not only when he is a boy but when he has grown to manhood. The Good Turn is one of the surest ways I know to overcome the human tendency to be selfish and to develop a habit as well as a capacity for thinking of others. The Good Turn spirit in the home is the basis for a happy home life. Every boy can reach that goal right now without waiting until he has grown up.

I have suggested here some big goals which are important for every boy. No doubt you will choose additional ones for yourself. The most important goal of all is one which makes all of the others worth while, and that is, the right kind of character. Your life work may become a mere chase for money or a matter of dull routine if you do not develop in yourself the qualities of mind that turn it into something worth while. Your hobbies may be just an excuse for selfishness if you do not share them with others and try to make them of some use to other people. And you can never hope for friends or a happy home if you do not build in yourself the Good Turn habit. Start now!

> *He only is a well-made man who has a good determination.*
>
> —EMERSON

STICK TO IT

EVERY outstanding permanent success to-day is, in my belief, based upon the ability to stick to the job, to push steadily on in spite of difficulties and hardships. Making a start—even a brilliant start—is not difficult. What counts is how you finish, and the thing that determines your success is your perseverance.

You will find this illustrated in the lives of men who have made their names famous. Thomas A. Edison was once a newsboy, but he had confidence in his ability, and he stuck to his job of inventing until he achieved success. Henry Ford was a humble machinist in Detroit, but he had a big idea. No one offered to help him, and his disappointments would have crushed a man of less determination. It was only his perseverance that carried him over his obstacles and over the top. Alexander Graham Bell, who invented the telephone, faced failure after failure, and was the laughing-stock of those who knew him. But he kept on in spite of discouragements until he perfected the invention that has benefited millions.

Many young people to-day have had so much done for them all their lives, have lived in comfortable homes and been sent to good schools, and had the advantages of easy living, that they have an idea that success is something that will come to them if they stand and hold out their hands to accept it. That is not so. Nothing that is worth having is gained without a struggle. But it is also true that nothing is impossible if you will only work for it persistently.

Of course, I mean work at it with intelligence. Don't attack a stone wall blindly and expect to knock it down by banging your head against it. Study the situation to find out the best spot to attack. Learn the most effective tools to use. Then go at it with all your might.

Many a man not especially gifted has achieved his outstanding success where others more brilliant have failed, simply because he kept plugging away. Defeat can not down you if you persevere. Don't give up. Don't be discouraged. Don't be diverted from what you set out to do. You can not fail if you stick to your undertaking. In accordance with your ability you are bound to reach your goal. Strike the word "impossible" out of your vocabulary.

When I was a young man a little pamphlet was published called, "A Message to Garcia." This was written by Elbert Hubbard about a true incident connected with the Spanish-American War. At that time it was necessary for President McKinley in Washington to get a message quickly to Garcia, the leader of the Insurgents, who was in an almost inaccessible place somewhere in the mountains of Cuba. No one knew where. A mail or telegraph message could not reach him. The message was entrusted to a young American. He asked no questions and received no instructions, but in four days he landed by night from an open boat off the coast of Cuba. He disappeared into the jungle. Three weeks later he reappeared on the other side of the island. He had crossed through unknown forests and difficult mountain paths, surrounded by hostile natives. He had delivered his message to Garcia!

In writing of this astonishing feat, Elbert Hubbard said, "It is not book learning young men need, nor instructions about this and that, but a stiffening of the vertebræ which will cause them to be loyal to a trust, to act promptly, concentrate their energies, do the thing. Civilization is one long anxious search for such individuals. He is needed and needed badly—the man who can 'carry a message to Garcia.'"

Happily, we can develop this quality in ourselves. It is something that every one of us in some measure can achieve, no matter what his other qualifications; and in achieving this, every boy has taken the first step along the road to achievement. Every boy has it in his power to be on the alert, to push forward bravely in spite of difficulties. Begin now in little things—your lessons at school, your tasks about the home, your activities in the playground, your Scout Troop and elsewhere. Not every boy can be brilliant or gifted, but this one important, essential thing he can learn—sticking to it.

> *Show me a young man who has not suc-*
> *ceeded at first, and nevertheless has gone*
> *on, and I will back that young man to do*
> *better than most of those who have suc-*
> *ceeded at the first trial.*
>
> —C. J. Fox

LUCKY BREAKS

SOME boys put a great deal of faith in what they call "Lucky Breaks." Some of them even think that without an unusual piece of good fortune they will never have a chance to get ahead in life. John D. Rockefeller working for $5.00 a week, Henry Ford starting in a power-house at $11.00 a week, Charles M. Schwab clerking in a grocery store—all of these were boys who "never had a chance." No, they never had a chance handed to them on a silver platter, but they went out on their own initiative and made themselves a chance. They fought against handicaps, they overcame obstacles. They accomplished what they set out to do.

"Lucky Breaks"? Abraham Lincoln was a bankrupt at twenty-two. The only assets he had in the world were his tools, and they were attached for debt. He was defeated again and again before he became President. Robert E. Fulton's first model of his steamship was a complete failure. Coming to more modern times, Paul Whiteman was once rejected because he could not play jazz; Ring Lardner was dismissed by an editor because he could not write.

Did these men sit around waiting for their luck to break? No, they started to work harder than ever on the basis of their experience and skill and energy and perseverance. Discouraged? Yes, undoubtedly, but defeat did not down them, and when the "lucky break" came they were ready. But all the lucky breaks in the world could not have lifted these men out of their slump. The men had to do that themselves.

Yes, "lucky breaks" do help, but no "lucky break" under the sun ever helped the man or boy who was not equipped within himself with the power to take advantage of it.

Don't worry about your "lucky break." Don't sit around now waiting for one to happen. Start out now to make it happen. The fellow who gets the "lucky break" in his examinations this month is the one who is making an effort to prepare himself now. You can't expect a "break" to do for you what you should do for yourself. The fellows who will step into the "swell jobs" and the "soft snaps," if you please, after they graduate from school and college are never going to hold them down unless they have equipped themselves during their boyhood with the skill and the knowledge and the fiber of character that will enable them to make good.

Moreover, for the young man who has ability, there are always chances. In a few years from now, the boys who read this page will be voting for a President; they will see in the newspapers the photograph of a great inventor; they will read the message of some man whose vision has brought benefits to thousands of people; they will hear about a financier who has built up a great industry; they will learn of a scientist who has successfully combated some baffling disease.

Right now these men are boys like yourself, going to the same type of school, studying the same lessons, perhaps from the same textbooks. Perhaps none of their teachers would single them out as more outstanding than you or thousands of boys like you. What will make the difference? A "lucky break"? Never believe it for a moment! It is what these boys are doing now, what they are building within themselves that is going to make that difference, ten, or twenty, or thirty years from now. You can't get ahead by sitting back and hoping for a "lucky break." You have to work constantly so as to be ready for it when it comes. There were never so many opportunities ahead for boys as there are right now. It is up to you to make the most of the ones that will undoubtedly come to you.

Now when we are all of us alive to the necessity for strengthening and invigorating democracy, it is more than ever important that each one of us try to do our share in the community, state, and nation. For most boys, doing their share will consist in equipping themselves to the very best of their ability with strong bodies, with education, and with right character so that they may, when the time comes, be able to take their share in the responsibilities of citizenship.

What happens to you in life depends on the whole, pretty much on what you yourself are and the character with which you have equipped yourself while you were a boy.

> *Luck is a very good word if you put a P before it.*
>
> —ANON

ASSETS AND HANDICAPS

HAVE you a handicap? Most of us have, of one kind or another. Sometimes it is something physical, sometimes it is economic, sometimes it is a handicap that we make for ourselves. But whatever the cause, it is not the handicap itself that matters; it is the way in which we work to beat it that counts. There are few handicaps that can not be turned into positive assets if we intensely desire to do so.

For example, most people know the story of Glenn Cunningham, the greatest champion runner of all times. He was so badly burned as a child that the doctors said he would never be able to walk again. He insisted on exercising his shriveled, tortured legs and turned his handicap into an asset. He not only developed health and strength, but he made himself a hero of the track and the idol of millions of boys.

A boy who suffered from a different kind of handicap was Harry. He came from a Children's Home in Chicago and his handicap was poverty. His clothes were queer, his manners were rough, and his chances to make something of himself seemed slim. Then some one invited him to join a Scout

Troop. The Institution authorities told him he could be a Scout if he didn't neglect his duties and if he kept up his school work. He joined the Troop and a new world opened.

He got permission from the Institution to take a paper route, and the first money he earned he spent for his Scout Uniform. When he met the other Scouts, outfitted just as they were, he no longer felt rough and awkward. He made friends. He advanced in Scouting and started his Merit Badge projects. Hard work? Of course. Lots of handicaps? Up before dawn to deliver his papers; back at the Home to do his chores; off to school, and then back for the rest of his duties. Hours snatched for study. Hours hoarded for his Troop Meetings and Scout work.

But gradually, out of it all, the vision of a larger world, and as the Merit Badge work continued, a dawning ambition. By the time he had earned his Eagle Badge, Harry knew what he was going to be, and he simply ignored his handicaps and forged ahead. He enlarged his paper route to earn more money for a technical education. He redoubled his efforts at school. It took a good many years, but he succeeded. To-day he has completed his technical training and his record was so outstanding, his courage and his perseverance so impressed the authorities, that they offered him a fine position in a hospital as medical technician, where he will have a chance to advance as far as his capacities permit, and to live a life of service to others.

Yes, there are few handicaps so serious that you can not overcome them if you really want to. The thing to do is to turn them into assets. Don't burden yourself with the needless handicaps of indecision, wobbly will-power and laziness. Have a goal! Decide what you want, and the steps to achieve it.

> *The block of granite which is an obstacle in the pathway of the weak, becomes a stepping-stone in the pathway of the strong.*
> —CARLYLE

LITTLE THINGS

SOMETIMES boys ask me about the different require-
ments in Scouting. Could they substitute something
for this one or that? It is a little thing. It does not
seem important.

Important! How can they know the importance
of apparently unimportant things?

Take the Tenderfoot Knots. Some years ago there
was a boy who wanted to be a Scout. The Scout-
master told him that he had to learn how to tie nine
kinds of knots. The boy did not particularly like to
do this, even the "Square Knot" which, as every
Scout knows, is a knot used for tying two ropes to-
gether.

"That's a 'Granny,'" his Patrol leader told him.
"Unless you bring the end of the left rope over,
down behind, and under the right end, you make a
'Granny,' and it pulls right out."

The boy wanted to be a Scout very much, so he
practiced until he could produce knots that passed
inspection. In his heart he felt he had not really
mastered his rope work. "As long as it gets by,
what's the difference?" he said to himself.

He joined the Troop. He became a member of a Patrol. He went to camp with the others and, as a result of his experience with this group, he began to consider more seriously the things he had learned and especially the First Scout Law, "A Scout is Trustworthy." Entirely on his own he went back to his Tenderfoot Knots and he practiced them until he knew in his heart that he was really proficient.

The rest of this story comes to me from the magazine section of the New York *Herald Tribune*, "This Week." A steeplejack got himself into a very tight place. By a series of accidents he was stranded at nightfall on a chimney two hundred feet up in the air, with no means of descent. It was dark. He had had a series of nerve-racking experiences in which his life had hung by a thread. Now he was clinging to the rim of the flue. In his exhausted and unnerved condition he could not hold onto his precarious perch much longer.

The whole town was watching his peril—watching in dead silence. When he had recovered some strength he called down for the tackle to be tied to his lead rope. Then he remembered something. The new lines in his tackle were not long enough to lower him the two hundred feet. He had plenty of spare line on the ground, but he had not spliced it to the new tackle.

He called down to ask if any one could make a

knot that would hold. There was a silence, and then somebody yelled up that they were sending for a **Boy Scout**.

After a while the Scout came, calling out that he could make a knot that he knew would hold. He tied the square knot and the rope began to run up. The steeplejack went over the edge into his "chair." He prayed all the way down that the Scout knew what he was talking about. The Scout did. The rope held and the steeplejack's feet touched the ground at last in safety. Men were shaking his hand, slapping his back. But one member of the crowd was in tears. It was the Scout who had tied the square knot.

Little things! Trifles! Dull stuff! Can you be sure? I always tell boys when they ask me about our Scout Requirements, that each one of them was adopted only after very careful, almost prayerful, consideration, with the definite purpose in the scheme of Scouting to equip a boy to take care of himself and others.

> *Every person is responsible for all the good within the scope of his abilities, and for no more, and none can tell whose sphere is the largest.*
>
> —GAIL HAMILTON

SMILE

ONE of the biggest assets a boy can have is a sincere smile. I do not know of anything that more enriches his personality, makes him attractive, and wins him friends. Why handicap ourselves needlessly by a forbidding manner? A little smile does a lot of good. Recently there came into my office, a young man with a business proposition. His proposition was sound and he talked well, but what impressed me was his smile. There is nothing more contagious than a smile.

When you smile something happens in your own heart and you pass something on to the other fellow. But be sincere about it. A smile is not just a twist of the lips. It shows what stuff a boy is made of. It can turn drudgery into a game. I know a boy who is clever and a good worker, but he plods glumly about his tasks. He is "fighting his pack." I know another boy who is not so clever, nor efficient, but his daily routine is an adventure. He whistles over the morning chores. When I meet him, his smile shows me that he has made his job a pleasure. If you were an employer, which of these boys would you engage?

A sincere smile shows ambition to get ahead, and the courage that laughs at obstacles. It shows imagination that turns a job into a game. It expresses friendliness, optimism, generosity, and an attractive personality.

There are times when a smile seems one of the hardest things to manage. That is when we need it most. During the first World War, some of our most popular songs were "smile songs." "Pack Up Your Troubles in Your Old Kit Bag, and Smile, Smile, Smile," sang the soldiers as they marched to the trenches.

Every boy has the opportunity of contributing his share toward making other people more happy. This he can do if he tries, and make himself the happier—by a smile. Cultivate the habit! A smile is the boy's Good Turn to the world. Practice cheerfulness. Merely to refrain from complaining is negative. Be positive, and smile. Let us do this not as a matter of form, but sincerely and naturally, because we have cultivated the habit. This is not a difficult thing to do. Experiment. Begin now, to-day. Especially when you meet some one disagreeable, smile, and watch his own expression change. When you tackle a disagreeable job try singing, and then smile. Lord Robert Baden-Powell said he found whistling was the best antidote for anger. Why not try? Resolve for one whole day to practice cheerfulness,

THE BOY WORTH WHILE IS THE SCOUT WITH A SMILE

Don't fight your pack, boys, don't fight your pack;
Take what is coming when you take the track:
It grows a little heavier and gets you in the back,
But go the miles with sunny smiles and don't fight your pack!

—DAVID STEVENS

and smiling. You can surely keep it up for one day
more—and then another—until you acquire the
habit. A smile is something that lies within the power
of every boy. We can not all be clever or talented.
We can not all be leaders. But we can be cheerful.
We can all smile. *Cultivate the habit.* Enrich your
personality and thus help spread sunshine and
happiness. A smile is a part of the Scout Law.

> *A Scout is cheerful. He smiles whenever*
> *he can. His obedience to orders is prompt*
> *and cheery. He never shirks nor grumbles*
> *at hardships.*
>
> —THE SCOUT LAW

ENTHUSIASM

EVERY worth-while achievement since the beginning of the world has been the result of some one's enthusiasm. Nothing can be accomplished without it. To have enthusiasm means to do everything that you undertake with all your might. This was the quality that Theodore Roosevelt had in mind when he said, "Hit the line hard, do not foul and do not flinch, but hit the line hard." Roosevelt himself was the very embodiment of enthusiasm. It was one of the outstanding qualities of his leadership. It was irresistible. He swept other people along with him, and by the sheer force of his enthusiasm, got things done that he had been told were impossible to accomplish.

Enthusiasm makes a monotonous job interesting. Without it we plod drearily through a task that often might be a real adventure. We must all of us submit to a certain amount of routine, and perform many tasks that in themselves are not especially interesting. But if we go at them with enthusiasm, with energy, and with cheerfulness we get our work done not only more efficiently, but with greater pleasure and profit to ourselves and others.

You have all of you known cases where a weak team defeated one apparently much stronger. But they could never have succeeded without enthusiasm. No indifferent or lazy team ever yet played in a championship game, and no indifferent or lazy man ever achieved real success.

I am not suggesting that a boy should pretend to feel something that he does not. Enthusiasm should be genuine and sincere. It is based on certain definite qualities. One of these is energy. The boy who drags around a listless, ailing body can not expect to feel much enthusiasm or interest in anything. I have often emphasized the individual responsibility of every boy to make and keep himself physically fit. It is my conviction, based on my experience, that most boys, with determination and a willingness to follow the simple rules prescribed, can make and keep themselves physically strong.

Another factor in enthusiasm is what I may term the right attitude of mind. It is an attitude that helps to overcome the human tendency to be selfish, and develop a habit as well as a capacity for thinking about other people. It is the fundamental spirit back of the Good Turn. Do not think about what you get out of a thing, but about what you put in. When next you have a disagreeable or monotonous job try going at it with a smile, and see how much easier it becomes. One of the biggest assets a boy can have is a sincere smile. It does a lot of good. It expresses friendliness, generosity, and the imagination that turns a job into a game. So, smile when you start a thing, go at it with all the energy that is in you, and you will find that you have developed genuine enthusiasm. Another thing—keep it up. It is not so hard to start things with enthusiasm. To carry them through, in the face of difficulties, involves real character.

I hope that every boy will, as a result of his experiences in school, at home, in church, and on the playground, develop in himself that quality of enthusiasm, and that he will, because of earnest and honest conviction, do everything that he undertakes with all his might. I hope that every boy will resolve first, last, and all the time to hit the line hard.

> *It is not the work, or the kind of work, but the spirit in which it is done that makes it free or servile, honorable, or degrading.*
>
> —DEAN INGE

PREPARED

THIS is a story of twenty-six rescues. It is a story of hazards and flood and fine courage. And yet to me, the outstanding thing is not the adventure, nor the courage, but the training that made it all possible. I do not believe that any ordinary group of boys could have made a record like this. But these Sea Scouts were prepared.

The story goes back to a year when heavy floods raged in New England. The section where the Sea Scouts lived was safe, but over the radio their Skipper learned of the plight of a town one hundred miles inland. He called the authorities and offered the services of his Sea Scouts and their boat. The authorities were skeptical about the usefulness of boys whose average age was barely seventeen, but they needed boats and trained men desperately, and they told the Skipper to come if he could get his boat and his Sea Scouts transported inland over one hundred miles of more or less impassable road.

From this point things moved with a rapidity that was possible only because careful plans had been made and tested for use in emergency. Through a prearranged mobilization system the Sea Scouts were rounded up, inside of twenty minutes, with the necessary equipment, and got the boat ready. Meantime, others were handling the problem of transportation. They needed a large truck to transport the boat and equipment. One source after another they tried but there was always a good reason why no truck was available for the hazardous trip. Finally, one owner said that the Scouts could have his large truck, but that it was already loaded with ten tons of green hides and the boys would have to unload the hides onto two smaller trucks. If you know anything about green hides you know that they are about as unpleasant a load as can be tackled.

After all, none of this was the Sea Scouts' business. They had offered their services and were prepared to do their part. The authorities had not been over-eager and nobody but themselves seemed to feel responsibility in the matter. I think that here is where an ordinary group might have gone off to bed feeling that they had done all that could be expected of them. But the Sea Scouts did not quit. They waded in. They unloaded the ten tons of green hides from the large truck to smaller ones. Midnight saw the job done; the boat was loaded on the big truck, and the group ready to roll. In a fog and a heavy rain they started into the darkness, through a flooded area that was so deep that the engine fan threw water out through the louvers on the side of the hood.

The rest of the story is a thrilling adventure that I can not tell in detail here. They reached their destination about dawn, unloaded their boat, and reported for duty. They rescued a sick man marooned in the second story of a house; a father and son who were floating down the river on a cake of ice and had been given up for lost. Twenty-six persons probably owe their lives to the training and courage of this group of boys. Finally, when the officials told them that all persons known to be in danger were accounted for, the boys called it a day. They loaded their truck and drove back home.

The adventure was thrilling. But do not forget the details that made it possible. Practice, patient practice to acquire the necessary skill in seamanship; a carefully developed plan of mobilization and service, perseverance in the face of difficulty, obstacles, and indifference. Finally, achievement and a service preëminently worth while.

> *Some men give up their designs, when they have almost reached the goal; while others, on the contrary, obtain a victory by exerting at the last moment, more vigorous efforts than before.*
>
> —SHAKESPEARE

WORK

EDISON once said that "Genius is one per cent inspiration and ninety-nine per cent perspiration." Perspiration—work! There never was an invention, or a discovery, or a worth-while achievement advancing the progress of the world that did not have some one's hard work as a basis.

The world to-day demands a far higher standard of efficiency than it used to. Our teachers must take a longer and more difficult training course than was thought necessary a generation ago; our doctors must be better prepared; our lawyers, yes, our bankers, our businessmen, must all be better qualified than formerly. The standards of the world are higher and it takes work to meet them, and to keep up with what is expected of us.

Why is it that some boys think of work as something unpleasant? I believe that one of the greatest joys of life is accomplishing something worth while, plugging away at a difficult job till it is finished successfully. You will find, if you ask them, that most of the successful men you know will tell you the experience that helped them most was the one that made them work the hardest.

Try to get the habit of work now, while you are young. To most of you this will involve your school studies. Pick your hardest course, and give it all you've got. Go at your algebra or your English lesson with the same effort and energy as if it were your one big opportunity, on which all your future success depended. Throw yourself into your church work, your home duties, your Scouting, in the same spirit. What you get out of them depends in a large measure on the good work that you put into them.

Opportunity means something, but work means more, and hard work often brings the opportunity when you least expect it. There are so many worthwhile things for you to do in the years ahead of you. Remember, the world has only just started on the road to advancement. Notice how every day some new record is broken, some new accomplishment is broadcast. Perhaps it may be only an athletic record, some pole-vaulter who jumps a fraction of an inch higher than the former champion, or a swimmer who knocks a few seconds off the previous record. Or it may be some extraordinary achievement like that of Admiral Byrd in the Antarctic.

All this should have a very definite meaning for the boys and young men of to-day. It should make them realize that there is still something worth while for every one of us to accomplish. The greatest inventions haven't yet been discovered; the greatest exploits haven't yet been carried through. In 1857 the Director of the Patent Bureau in Washington resigned because he thought there could be no more inventions made that would be worth his time and effort! There are still hundreds of glorious achievements ahead of us which the world does not even dream of to-day. They are worth working for, aren't they?

I hope that in your thoughts of your future work you are remembering that it is rare to get satisfaction out of working for ourselves alone. We must work for others as well. Indeed, one of the most important factors in the education of any person is to give him as a goal, a desire to be of service to others. It matters not much what this service shall be, if it be a genuine service for some one, beyond self.

How I wish that more young men would realize this! Our whole Scouting program was very definitely planned to offset the human tendency of each of us to be selfish. We try to develop a capacity and a habit of caring for others. Only in so far as you boys and young men of America do work hard, and keep in mind the goal of greater service to others, will you achieve worth-while success.

> *It is not joy nor repose which is the aim*
> *of life. It is work, or there is no aim at all.*
> —AUERBACH

KNOWING HOW

THIS is a true story about what happened in a family in Muskogee, Oklahoma.

It was winter, very cold, and on this particular morning a gas-heater had been lighted to warm the little group while they were dressing. They were playing around as young children do and one of them thoughtlessly stepped too close to the gas-heater. In an instant, her flimsy night clothes were a mass of flames! The little girl shrieked and the other children began to cry. The mother came running, and stood filled with horror. The father and thirteen-year-old son came dashing up the stairs. The son was a Boy Scout and in his Troop he had often practiced, as part of his First Aid training, responding to just such accidents. Almost automatically he caught up a small rug from the floor, and rolled his shrieking little sister in its enveloping folds. In a moment, he had smothered the flames and had prevented serious injury!

The next day the father told the boy's Scoutmaster about what had happened, and said, "Thank God, my son is a Scout and has learned First Aid! He

59

knew what to do while I stood helplessly confused."

Here is another story about a Scout. He was so freckled that the boys called him Turkey Egg. He had a buddy named Bob.

When the incident happened it was vacation time and Bob had a job working at the bottle-capping machine in a soft-drink factory. One day something went wrong and there was an explosion. The crash of a burst bottle; and a sliver of a razor-sharp glass flew out and cut Bob's wrist. Bright blood spurted out; an artery was severed!

Everybody ran around in circles. Somebody thought to telephone the doctor of the little town, but he was out on a call. Severe arterial bleeding can cause the victim to bleed to death in only a few minutes—certainly before the doctor could be summoned. Nobody knew what to do.

Then, in rushed Turkey Egg! Turkey Egg knew his First Aid. He sized up the situation; caught up a handkerchief and with that and a lead pencil, applied a tourniquet. He had one of the men hold it; got a roll of clean gauze bandage from the company's First Aid kit; put a compress over the wound; held the arm up with the help of a sling, tightened and loosened the tourniquet as needed. At last the doctor arrived and took charge. Said he, "A mighty good job. The boy is alive only because this Scout knew his First Aid."

KNOWING HOW

Work that is play to a Boy Scout.

I receive in my office hundreds and hundreds of records like this, showing where human lives have been saved because some Scout knew his First Aid. I regard a knowledge of First Aid as one of the most practical pieces of training a boy can secure. Every boy whether he is a Scout or not should equip himself with a knowledge of First Aid. Such training will be of lasting benefit. It may be needed with utter unexpectedness. Emergencies and accidents requiring knowledge of First Aid occur daily in the home, playground, and on the streets.

We in Scouting give boys training in First Aid as part of their requirements, but there are agencies in practically every community that will help you to organize a class if you are really interested. The boy who makes good on the job is one who uses common sense and keeps his head. That is just as important as knowing what to do. Usually the first aider is on the job ahead of the doctor and upon his knowledge and judgment may depend the safety and even the life of the victim. Surely there is no greater satisfaction that any of us can feel than the knowledge that we have been instrumental in saving a human life, and surely, there is nothing that can give us more basis of confidence and self-reliance than the knowledge that we are qualified to render this service.

Every boy should equip himself to be of service

to himself and others with a thorough knowledge of First Aid. Those of us who are Scouts are obligated on our honor to do our best to be helpful to others at all times. Furthermore, we work under the Scout Motto "Be Prepared" and therefore it is our responsibility to take full advantage of the instruction in First Aid which the Scout Program makes available in order that we may be prepared, alert and qualified to be helpful to others.

> *Here is a good definition of First Aid— if you are asked for one. It is the emergency treatment given in cases of injury or illness when a doctor is needed—before he arrives, and also: the immediate care of slight injuries. First Aid is not doctoring or nursing. IT IS ONLY FIRST CARE. If further aid is needed it should be given by a physician.*
>
> —HANDBOOK FOR BOYS

BOOKS

MY interest in books and the value of reading is a real and vital thing because I know from actual, first-hand experience what reading can do for a boy. Reading has been one of the most determining factors in my life.

I lost my parents in early childhood and was placed in an orphan home. Furthermore, in my early years there developed a tubercular trouble in my hip and knee. At the age of eight I was a piece of human wreckage classified as hopeless, useless material by two fine institutions.

For years I remained in the orphanage without relatives, or special friends of any kind, and then a good Christian woman became interested in my case because she had known my mother. She tried to do something for me. Finally she gave me one of her own books to read. Later she asked me questions about the characters in it, and started me to thinking about them in a constructive way. There was a small library, long unused at the orphanage. In my new enthusiasm, I got the matron to open it and let me read. More than that, I arranged so that the other children could use the books. At first, I had to offer from my meager resources a cent for every book read, and secure permission for those reading to remain up an extra hour at night.

I started to public school. By the time I was sixteen, I had read, without exaggeration, every book on which I could get my hands—Cooper, Dickens, Scott, Gibbon's *Decline and Fall of the Roman Empire* entire, if you please, Macaulay and Victor Hugo, Shakespeare and others. The institution routine made it necessary for me not only to read the Bible, but commit to memory many chapters and verses. The daily newspaper played its part in my education and character formation. There was only one paper that come to the orphanage, and I had to get up early in the morning to read it before any one else wanted it, and be sure to fold it carefully again in the same creases, so as not to leave it rumpled.

That is why my interest in books and reading for young people has always been so personal and vital, and that is why, as a part of my responsibility for leadership in the Boy Scouts of America, one of the first things I did was to promote a reading program. No one thing, among many, in my judgment, is so much a factor for influencing attitude of mind and daily habits of conduct upon which we depend for our character development.

Tell me what a boy reads and how he spends his leisure time, and I can tell you what he will probably become. Boys who spend hours reading what is often called "trash"—books that are carelessly written and inaccurate, books with characters that are not true to life—rarely develop into leaders. In later life they are incapable of forming clear, independent judgments; they can be led about like sheep just as, when they were boys, the trash they read led them about like sheep. The reason for this is obvious. Each one of us has only one mind. A boy doesn't have one mind that he reads with, and another that he plays ball with. A man runs his business, and makes his investments, with the same mind that he read books with when he was a boy.

This makes reading worth-while books tremendously important. Good habits of observation and comparison, checking up with facts to see that they are accurate, comparing characters in books with characters met in real life, result from reading good literature.

Of course you read. Every boy does. Be sure to make a balanced ration of good reading that provides for the solid things that build mind and character, as well as those that are only entertaining.

Even in small communities there is usually one public library. Get acquainted with your local librarian and ask for suggestions on worth-while reading. Take out a membership card. Talk to your school teacher and to others who may be qualified to advise you about books, or lend them to you. Start a library of your own, even if you can afford only a few books.

> *Learn to be discriminative in your reading; to read faithfully, and with your best attention, all kinds of things which you have a real interest in—a real, not an imaginary—and which you find to be really fit for what you are engaged in.*
>
> —CARLYLE

HOBBIES

THE boy who has a hobby has more adventure in a day than the dull boy does in a year. He has more friends. Interesting things are always happening to him. Every day he plunges into some new undertaking.

A hobby is something that you do because you want to. Don't spend your spare time aimlessly loafing and lounging. Get a hobby and have some fun!

Get a hobby and have some friends! You will make them faster than you ever did in your life before. With a hobby you are more interesting to other people. Other people interest you more.

What do you like to do, to make, to collect, to study? The world is so full of worth-while things that there is no possible excuse for any one ever being bored or lonely.

Don't choose all of your hobbies along the same line. If you are interested in stamp collecting try to learn something about radio. If you like to carve wood, learn how to bind books. If you are interested in collecting rocks and minerals, make a hobby of tennis or skating or some outdoor sport as well. In this way you will have a chance to find out the kind of thing that you can really do most readily and with greatest satisfaction to yourself.

A hobby gives you a chance to become really an authority on some one thing. Don't think that I am saying too much when I make this statement. It is actually within the power of most boys, with study and perseverance, enthusiasm and effort, really to become authorities on a subject that interests them. You can read books in a public library in most communities. There are museums and collections that can be visited. There is usually some one who is an authority in or near your own community on the subject that interests you. Ask him questions, ask other people questions. Keep on digging and finding out more and more about your hobby.

Many boys of your age have been experts, who had no better advantages than you. John Ericsson, who invented the monitor, began inventing at eleven; George Stephenson, who invented the locomotive, got his first idea for a steam-engine at fifteen; Tennyson published poetry at eighteen; McCormick invented the reaper at twenty-two, and Howe the sewing-machine at twenty-six. Galileo, the astronomer, invented a clock pendulum at eighteen years of age. Agassiz began his scientific career at eleven.

Perhaps your hobby involves skill. Here is a

chance for you really to excel. Patience and perseverance! There is no reason why you should not become really expert. I have seen marvelous woodcarvings done by Scouts as a part of their Merit Badge work. We have Olympic champions in their teens, major-league baseball players who are not yet old enough to vote. It is all up to you. During the Battle of Britain, England was defended by an air force composed of young men whose average age was nineteen.

What's your hobby? Make a success of it! The extent of your success will be measured by what you, yourself, really are and what you put into it, and your rewards will be accordingly. Don't be stingy in what you try for! Give everything you've got and you will find that your entire life will be richer and happier.

> *Learning in the truest sense of the word, is not merely something acquired. Mere knowledge, in great abundance and variety, may, to be sure, be taken up by the mind, as a sponge takes up water; but learning which deserves the name, is quite a different achievement.*
> —ROSWELL D. HITCHCOCK

WELL AND STRONG

WHY not make a hobby of health? Every boy wants to be physically strong. It makes possible efficiency, effectiveness, and, indeed, happiness. A healthy body with no remediable defects uncorrected is the basis for every worth-while achievement. With it go mental alertness and high character. To be physically strong does not mean that one has to be a giant with bulging muscles, who devotes most of his time to developing a physique that is useful only in some form of athletic competition. I mean rather, that every boy should have his body under control, that he should be supple and quick and easy of movement, with strong heart and lungs. Such a body as this helps him to achieve, to carry through what he undertakes, and to make his life successful.

This kind of strength, physical fitness, is based upon an intelligent understanding, on the part of the boy, that he is the trustee of his own physical being. He does not need to become a star athlete, or spend long hours in the gymnasium or on the football field. It is not muscular development that is most important, but the strengthening of the vital organs, such as the heart and lungs, and developing, not big muscles, but strong muscles, that respond quickly to his will.

In Scouting we emphasize strength. It is a part of the Scout Oath, and Scout activities are designed to help to develop it. We urge boys to have a thorough physical or health check-up once or twice a year. We endeavor to inform them of the simple rules of proper diet and play and exercise, and encourage them to secure regular and sufficient sleep, fresh air, sunlight, and develop cleanliness of body within and without, regular habits of work and study, good posture and a joyful and happy attitude toward life. These should be a matter of definite planning on the part of every boy until they become daily habits.

Camping is a wonderful aid in developing a strong, sturdy body. Indeed, there is no more joyful and effective method, especially when you make it an adventure. You can do it, no matter where you live or what your circumstances, if you use imagination. Try being a backwoodsman. Get out in the open. In the open you learn things first-hand instead of out of books. Give yourself a chance to learn by doing. Don't limit yourself just to sports, but deliberately set yourself to learn something about nature. Explore the stars overhead. Learn something about trees. Study the wild animals in the woods—

or birds—or insects—or fishes—whatever interests you, and give yourself the adventure of first-hand study and observation.

I know of nothing that helps to develop a boy's self-reliance, courage, endurance, and ambition more than adventure in the out-of-doors. Never shall I forget my first experience at a camp-fire held shortly after I came into the Boy Scout Movement. The leader in perfectly good faith wished that I should have the honor of lighting the camp-fire, and he, much to my amazement and embarrassment—and I thought "finish"—handed me a fire-making set and told me to go to it. The only experience I had ever had was to see some one else do this once or twice before. (Those were the early days of Scouting and fire-making was not as common then as now.) It was a momentous occasion in my life, but I did it, believe it or not, without a hitch, and without undue delay.

I wish that every one of you could have at least one such experience as that—the satisfaction of accomplishing something that you did not know how to do before.

Action may not always bring happiness; but there is no happiness without action.
                                        —DISRAELI

IT CAN BE DONE!

THIS is a story which goes beyond one person's record of achievement. It is a story of a boy who overcame his own handicaps and brought the opportunity for achievement to a whole group of boys who were similarly handicapped. It is as stirring, as colorful a story as any that have come to me in Scouting. It is a story of a crippled boy, yes a whole Troop of crippled boys, who became Scouts and Sea Scouts.

It has its beginning when Emmett Sherlock became a Scout. A victim of paralysis, this youngster of fourteen was a Scout in a Troop of boys with all their normal faculties. He enjoyed Scouting and became a First-Class Scout. But he had in his mind that other crippled boys whom he knew, boys in the school for crippled boys which he attended, ought to have the advantage of Scouting. This youngster of only fourteen heard of a group of businessmen on the west side of Chicago whom he thought might sponsor a Troop. Bravely this boy went to them and challenged them to serve the crippled youth of Chicago: "This is what we need. What will you do

73

about it?" They responded, and to-day two Troops of Scouts and a Sea Scout Ship stand as a tribute to this lad's interest.

The story of Emmett Sherlock is interesting also because of what Emmett did personally to overcome his handicaps. Swimming held him back for a long time. It is true that many crippled persons are strong swimmers, but in Emmett's case it took months of patient and determined effort to make his twisted body master the water. He finally succeeded and became, as I have said, a First Class Scout. But he could not pass the Life Saving test that is required for Eagle Scout Rank. He went to camp summer after summer, trying to achieve it, without success. Finally after many years of effort, he finally succeeded, and, thrilled with the anticipation of receiving the coveted Eagle Badge, he returned to his home.

Unfortunately, fate interfered with his plans and Emmett never received the Eagle Badge while he was living, for he died of pneumonia a month after he returned from camp. But his friends helped to pin upon his breast the Eagle Badge which he had so bravely won, and which was a tribute to that spark of "It Can Be Done."

In his short lifetime he had accomplished more in mastering himself, and in service to others than many who live three times his years. The boy who was a victim of a hopeless and crippling disease, by perseverance earned his Life-Saving Merit Badge and qualified himself to save the lives of others. The boy whose physical handicaps were such that he could not attend a school for normal boys, brought the activities of normal boyhood, camping, and the life of the open fields and woods, to handicapped inmates of his school.

Isn't this the most convincing proof that it is not what happens to you, but the way which you take it, that determines what your life will be? There is joy, adventure and infinite opportunity for service for those who will accept the challenge.

People do not lack strength; they lack will.
—Victor Hugo

OBEDIENCE

THE bronze hum of an airplane high overhead. The Air Mail winging its way through the night. In clear sky through banks of clouds, across rivers and mountain chains, over cities and fields, these messengers cleave the way to their objective. There is drama and romance in their magnificent performance. Free as a bird they seem, flying like a bird high in the sky.

Free, yes, but the secret of their freedom, as of all freedom, is Obedience. Obedience to laws; to laws of nature, laws of mankind, and laws of mechanics.

The Air Mail has run up a glorious record on maintaining their schedule. In spite of well-nigh insurmountable obstacles they carry on and get there *On Time*. It is a wonderful example of Obedience. Obedience to Duty as well as to Orders.

These heroes of the air, the Air Mail pilots, couldn't even take their ships off the ground if their eyes and hands and feet were not trained to Obedience. Obedience to their Will, the orders of their judgment.

A liner runs into a storm at sea. A driving gale

beats it far off its course. Seas running mountain high toss it about like a chip. There comes a sickening lurch and the lights go out. All hands are called to the life-boats. Half the boats can not be launched for the starboard list. Two of the other boats are swamped. An explosion is feared. Pandemonium reigns. Men and women turn animal, forgetful of all the inhibitions of civilization. They claw and trample and thrash around, endangering their own safety and that of others.

But there are a number of heroes there, quietly and efficiently going about what is to be done, thoughtful of others, and of the decencies of life. They are the ones who save the lives of others, and their own, too. What makes them Heroes? It is this: they have trained themselves to discipline of mind and action and obedience, and when a crisis comes they are masters of themselves. That is Obedience!

A parent gives a command, the reason for which is not apparent. Scoutmaster or Patrol Leader issues an order. What is this thing called Obedience? The pleasing of a loved one; the respect to a duly constituted authority; the conforming to a recognized organization. All these things, perhaps, but far more, too. It is the building up of a self-discipline that is the very essence of Heroism.

As the pilot's hand on the control stick and his foot on the rudder bar are trained to such obedience that their action seems an unconscious reaction, so your obedience is building up mental discipline that will stand you in good stead all your life.

It is the habit of Obedience or discipline of mind and actions in little things that gives one that personal quality which makes possible the doing of big or worth-while things.

Obedience and discipline are things which we all have to learn. The boy who is fortunate enough to learn them in his youth, incident to his daily routines in the commonplace things of the home and school life, is spared some very hard knocks when he grows older. Intelligence, skill—these are fine qualities to have, but, unless a boy has learned how to make them obey his will, they will not do him much good. Discipline is necessary everywhere.

The thing is to coöperate happily in the process which develops discipline and obedience in the doing of small things while we are young. Then, when our turn comes to do big things, discipline will help to insure accomplishment. Often a boy must obey as a matter of duty when he would rather be doing something else. When he has learned to obey orders cheerfully, he is well along on the road to a life full of satisfaction and usefulness.

> *Obedience alone gives the right to command.*
>
> —EMERSON

TAKE HOLD

It isn't always the headlines that count. Few of us make headlines, or get a chance to be heroes. Character and Scout training count, however, in a small emergency, just as in a spectacular adventure.

There was that party of Iowa Scouts, for instance, who started off from camp on a hike. A couple of hours later a runner dashed back to camp with news. The hikers had come upon a horse helpless, mired down in the soft mud on the south trail. The horse had evidently been struggling there for two or three days for it was completely exhausted, famished and thirsty. Planking embedded in the mud about the poor animal showed some one had tried a rescue but failed.

The Patrol Leader sent the runner back to camp with instructions, then collected canteens, crept carefully out to the planking and poured water into the mouth of the horse, who gulped it gratefully. Meantime, when the runner reached camp with the news, a second Patrol gathered spades and a long tug-of-war rope, put them into a big canoe, and set off by the shorter water route.

When they reached the scene, the Patrol Leader carried one end of the rope out to the horse, turned to the Scouts and asked what kind of knot should be used. They made it unanimous for a bowline to be tied about the horse's neck. The Scouts lined up and at the command gave a mighty heave. That did it, and the horse was able to scramble weakly to its feet and stagger away, none the worse for its experience.

Nothing especially dramatic about that. But consider what those Scouts revealed! A spirit of kindness and helpfulness, first; skill, knowing the right kind of knot for the purpose; democratic coöperation to work together; leadership to plan and direct. Victories have been won on less.

Coöperation is a fine thing, but there are times when we have to think quickly alone, like the Scout from Fort Snelling, Minnesota, at the Council's Annual Round-Up. There were seven thousand spectators, and four thousand Scouts in a circus program. This Scout's humble job was to carry placards, prepared for him in advance, around the arena advising the Scouts on the sidelines when to assemble, and what they should do in each of the acts.

The grand finale of the show was a salute to the Flag as it was lowered, and all the Scouts and the spectators were supposed to stand. If anything had gone wrong, it would have spoiled the fundamental purpose of the whole demonstration, which was to show Scout Citizenship. The Scout picked up his placard, looked at it and instead of starting around the arena, raced to the program director, for the placard read through some error, "Scouts and audience be seated." The Scout verified the error, grabbed a marking crayon, quickly lettered a new sign and dashed out into the arena.

Why do I think this story ranks with many that make headlines? In the first place, because the Scout did not work like a machine. Although he had a routine job when others were doing spectacular stunts for the public, he put intelligence and observation into it. Next, he had knowledge—he knew his Flag Code. Knowledge gave him confidence. But he still had responsibility to others who knew more. He must check. Then he showed skill and initiative to repair the error. Qualities like these carried Livingstone through darkest Africa.

All around us are opportunities to take hold and do! No boy need feel that because he has not yet reached voting age he can not make his influence felt in the community. Every day opportunity awaits you if you will accept it. Every day you are being tested. You can serve not alone through Scouting and its civic-service program, but through church, school, grange, neighborhood, and other clubs. The aim of the Boy Scout Movement is to give you personal help in the building of your character and training yourself for citizenship. Every day all over the country on thousands of occasions that never make the headlines, Scouts demonstrate participating citizenship.

> *Success is the sum of detail. If one attends only to the great things and lets the little ones pass, the great things become little and failure follows.*
> —HARVEY S. FIRESTONE

CITIZENS

I THINK it is fairly universally recognized that a Scout, by his special experience and training, has acquired a definite and distinctive citizenship advantage in the scheme of things as they are to-day. He has accepted the personal responsibility to plan his daily life and actions so as to keep himself physically strong, mentally awake and morally straight! The Boy Scout need not wait until he reaches voting age to make his influence felt as a sturdy, loyal citizen. Indeed, no boy need wait until he is of voting age to "take hold" as a citizen. There are abundant opportunities for service, not alone through Scouting and its civic-service program, but through church, school, grange, neighborhood, and other groups.

Be constantly alert for opportunities to coöperate and render service. Cultivate your capacity to understand and care about other people. Be tolerant and respect the rights of others. Develop courage, self-reliance. Be vigilant in showing by your speech and action your faith in America, your faith in God. As Scout Citizens, accept your responsibility for extending among those with whom you come in contact their understanding and appreciation of the ideals of Scouting and the principles that have made us, and will always keep us, a great democracy.

The aim of the Scout Movement has been to give you personal help in the building of your character and in training yourself for citizenship, and now you are called upon to serve as "participating citizens." Throughout the ages, the Athenian Oath has served a useful purpose in stirring people everywhere to better citizenship. In this spirit, if you are fifteen years of age and over, I recommend for your individual consideration and voluntary action, in addition to maintaining your obligation under the Scout Oath, or Promise and Laws, the following Senior Scout Citizenship Dedication to which I gave considerable attention to developing in connection with our new Manual, *Adventuring for Senior Scouts:*

1. I will continue to live the Scout Oath and Law.

2. I will keep myself familiar with the Declaration of Independence and the Constitution of the United States—with its Bill of Rights and obligations.

3. I will respect and obey the law—to further that true freedom and security for all, which comes with liberty under law.

4. I will wholeheartedly coöperate in the responsibilities of my home, and will participate in the civic and social activities of my school, church, neighborhood, and community, and when legally qualified, I will regularly register and vote in community, state, and national elections.

A SCOUT IS LOYAL

He is loyal to all to whom loyalty is due, his Scout leader, his home, and parents and country.

5. I will deal fairly and kindly with my fellow citizens of whatever race or creed, in the spirit of the Twelfth Scout Law and its faith in God, and America's guarantee of religious freedom.

6. I will work for America and will guard our heritage —its liberties and responsibilities—realizing that the privileges we enjoy to-day have come as a result of the hard work, sacrifice, faith, and clear thinking of our forefathers, and I will do all in my power to transmit our America, reinforced, to the next generation.

We place these things before you confident that you will keep the fine spirit of American reverence, tolerance, and loyalty burning in your life as a "participating citizen," who cares about his fellow citizens and seeks to "help other people at all times." That spirit is the life blood of America. Guard it and live it!

> *"One flag, one land, one heart, one hand,*
> *One Nation evermore!*
> —OLIVER WENDELL HOLMES

MAKING GOOD

THIS happened in Sequoia National Park. A forest fire was raging. Everybody in the community was out fighting the fire. On a hill was a band of forest service men who suddenly found themselves in a desperate situation—trapped by a ring of flames on all sides. No chance to telephone, of course. Too far to shout.

The imperiled rangers began to send out frantic SOS signals with their signal flags for more water and more men.

But nobody paid the slightest attention to them! Every one in the vicinity was fighting the fire elsewhere, though not in such terrible danger.

In one party of fire-fighters, however, was a Scout. His attention was caught by the signals. He was *the only one in the entire party of sixty who could read the message*. He rounded up the rest of the party, who went to the rescue of the trapped men, and they were saved just in time.

A knowledge of signaling is a part of the outdoorsman's equipment, just as are his pack and his ax. Not only Scouts use it, but National Guardsmen,

forest rangers, surveyors, and engineers, sailors—
all pioneers, whether on sea or land. In the Battle
of Britain, lives have depended on it. It is essential
in all kinds of emergencies.

There are fine traditions about signaling. In Bib-
lical times signals were sent by fires. Greeks and
Romans used torches. Among the savage tribes of
the north, beacon fires were lighted on the hills for
signals. Our American Indians signaled with smoke,
and the native Africans with tomtoms. It is said
that when King George V of England passed away,
it was known to the savages in darkest Africa before
many white men learned of it. Even wild animals
use signals.

To me there is no activity more Scoutlike than
signaling. It smacks of the open, the wilderness
camp, the untrod trail, and the wide sky. Stuffy
rooms and steam heat, telephone service, and me-
chanical gadgets just don't go with signal flags. It
is a fresh-air, an adventurous, a primitive game.

During a disastrous flood, when the Ohio River
overflowed its banks, Scout signalers again proved
their worth. The city of Zanesville, Ohio, is divided
in two by the river, which flows through the heart
of the city. On this occasion, all telephone and tele-
graph wires were torn down, and the city was left
stranded without light or communication. The first
communication that was established between the

two halves of the city was by two Troops of Scouts on either bank of the Ohio River, who signaled messages across to each other.

It is fun to be able to send messages to some one a mile away perhaps—messages in code that ordinary people can not read.

Like other things, how much you enjoy it depends upon how well you can do it. Whether you use General Service or the Semaphore Code, signal flags, or a flashlight, you have to be good, or it is no use to you. In Scouting we include signaling in the Scout requirements because it is part of the equipment of outdoorsmen and because we believe it helps a boy to be accurate, painstaking, and thorough. We feel signaling is really essential if the Scout is to stand on his own feet and take care of himself in the open, and be prepared to help other people at all times.

Signaling can be useful in most unexpected emergencies. One evening one of our Scouts saw an airplane circling over his town. He suddenly noticed that it was flashing a light. As he watched, he made out the signals. "N-A-M-E," the pilot was flashing. The Scout was quick-witted and guessed that the aviator had lost his way and was asking for information. He rushed into the house, got a large mirror, ran out, turned on the lights of an automobile that was parked near-by, and held the mirror so that the beam of light was reflected upward. In long and short flashes he signaled the name of the town. The pilot answered, "T-H-A-N-X," and flew away into the night.

> Out in the woods where telephones and telegraph messengers are not to be had, some method of signaling is essential. If different parties are hunting for a lost person, for example, signaling enables them to work together—advise when found and so on.
>
> —HANDBOOK FOR BOYS

FRIENDLY

A FUNDAMENTAL part of the game of Scouting is that it gives a boy a chance to do worth-while things with other Scouts as a member of a Patrol or Troop. He is a member of a group to which he acts loyally, in which he should take pride, and for which he will work with other Scouts. More than that, all members of his Troop are on the same footing. Your clothes in your school may, because of economic conditions, be better than the other fellow's, or you may have patches on the seat of your trousers. But as a Scout you are in the Uniform of the Scout. And there you put in operation a tremendous force for building friendships.

One of the most important assets any boy can have is the ability to make friends. This applies not only when he is young, but when he is a man as well.

The capacity to get along well with people, to avoid friction and promote good will and cheerfulness, helps us to make effective use of our abilities. Yes, it is essential to success in practically every walk of life. Every boy, whether he is a Scout or not, ought to cultivate the habit of friendliness in the same way that we do in Scouting, sharing his interests and his good times with others on a basis of democracy.

More than this, he should look for opportunities to be helpful to his friends. What is the evidence of friendliness? What is the test of a friendship? The fact that an individual cares for something beyond himself. He is unselfish, he cares for his friends sufficiently to want to be of help to them. His attitude of mind is such that he feels an obligation not only to carry his own pack, but to be anxious at least to help carry some one else's pack.

The friendly boy is coöperative in school with the group. He does his full share to make a success of any enterprise of which it is a part—to help make the team win, for instance, not to glorify himself as a star, not from a selfish motive, but because he is a loyal friend and a member of the group.

I can think of no place where a boy has a better opportunity to practice friendliness than in camp. The whole camp idea is based on team work, foregoing your selfish inclinations, for the welfare of others. This is one of the rules of the game. The "Buddy System," a plan which has been developed in Scout Camps for the greater safety of swimmers, illustrates the value of friendship. During the swimming period each boy swims with a Buddy. Should he get into difficulty, his Buddy would help him and call others to his assistance. The safety and advantages of the swimming period are more than helped by this simple form of coöperation. In the same way you will find that all your experiences become much more worth while if you share them with your friends.

Tolerance is involved in friendship, and that wonderful thought in the Twelfth Scout Law, "He . . . respects the convictions of others in matters of custom and religion." The things we have in common with other people are much more important than the things which we have not. To make friends, learn to look below the surface differences to the things in which you are really alike.

On the foundation of friendliness and tolerance the Scout Movement has built a brotherhood that reaches around the world. Every boy, however, can cultivate these qualities for himself and make his own life richer and happier as well as of more service to others.

> *A Scout is friendly. He is a friend to all*
> *and a brother to every other Scout.*
> —FOURTH SCOUT LAW

CHRISTMAS SPIRIT

THEY lived in a small wooden house in New London. Even the oldest, a little girl of ten, failed to realize the plight of the family caused by their father's accident. All the children were confident that Santa Claus would fill their stockings while they slept on Christmas Eve.

To the mother the situation was desperate, because her little family of seven needed food and clothing, and there were long weeks ahead before her injured husband would be discharged from the hospital. While the children were chattering of roller skates, dolls, and Christmas trees, she was trying to figure out how to scrape together enough to keep the home going.

Then there came a knock on the door. "Santa Claus!" shouted the youngest. It was not Santa Claus, but a Boy Scout with a smile extending clear across his face. In his arms a bag overflowed with toys. Behind him stood another Scout and another— a whole Troop of Boy Scouts, bringing toys and provisions and clothing, enough to carry the family through the weeks ahead; for the Troop had adopted this family as their Good Turn. **Christmas was a joyous day in that family, after all.**

This is only one of hundreds of reports that were made to me of Christmas Good Turns in one year. One Troop in Massachusetts visited a Children's Hospital and presented an entertainment for the children and gave them presents. Many gave Christmas parties to less-chance children. Often they performed cheerfully and willingly difficult jobs for other organizations. Out in Ohio, Scouts made a house-to-house canvas for old books and magazines that were to be used by a local organization as Christmas presents.

The Scout Executive in Lewistown, Pennsylvania, wrote me a very interesting story. It was cold on Christmas Eve and at half-past eight he had settled down to enjoy Christmas Eve with his own family, when the door-bell rang. There he found two cold Scouts and a truck driver, who had been out in an open truck since early afternoon, with thirty baskets to deliver for an organization. They had been unable to locate two of the families on the list that had been given them from the agency. But it never occurred to the Scouts to leave those families with no Christmas dinner. They drove to the Scout Office and it was closed, so they hunted up the Scout Executive and came to him for better instructions. He did a little telephoning and then the Scouts got on the job again.

Of all the Good Turns reported to me I take a special interest in the project of collecting and repairing and distributing toys. For weeks before Christmas, many Troops conduct a systematic canvas for broken or discarded toys. Then they set up their toy shop. No toy is too small to be accepted. The utmost care and thought are given to make the toys new and shiny again, it is reported. This is a project which is carried out with joy to the Scouts as well as to children who might otherwise have no Christmas toys.

In Herkimer, New York, there was a Troop composed almost completely of foreign-born boys who were in a position to be receivers of gifts rather than givers. And yet, as early as October, these boys were making personal visits to well-to-do families, collecting toys, reconditioning them, and planning to redistribute them. First their goal was one hundred and fifty toys, but they found that too easy and reached it by the end of the first month. Then they raised the mark to three hundred and passed that. Once more it was raised to five hundred and later to one thousand. Toys were distributed just before Christmas. When the Scouts went home they felt that the things that had made their Christmas brightest were the smiles and the joyous shouts of the children to whom they had played Santa Claus.

Our Scout Law says that "A Scout is Helpful," stressing his obligation to be helpful at all times. But at Christmas, he should have a definite, planned program of helpfulness. If not in coöperation with his Troop, then on his own, for every boy during the Christmas Season has at least some time that he can devote to service for others. I urge every Scout to make a comprehensive plan to be unselfishly thought out and executed. If he does, I am sure at the end of Christmas Day he will be happier because of the fact that his giving of himself in expression and actual gifts will exceed what he will receive.

> *Men of the noblest dispositions think themselves happiest when others share their happiness with them.*
>
> —JEREMY TAYLOR

HOME

A GOOD home is one of the most important influ-
ences in a boy's life. Some boys just take their homes
for granted. If you want to find out what a good
home really means, ask the boy who hasn't one. One
of our Scout Executives once asked this question of
young men in a State Reformatory in Rhode Island,
and seventy-five per cent of them told him that they
had not had a proper home life. Some people in a
position to know say as high as ninety-five per cent
of our criminals had the wrong kind of home in-
fluences. So evidently right home training does
count!

I do not mean, of course, that you will neces-
sarily become a criminal, if you fail to appreciate
your home. But I do mean—and how I wish it were
possible for me to meet face to face every boy who
reads this page, so that I could present this chal-
lenge to him personally—I do mean that every boy
will grow into a better man—yes, a happier man
and a better citizen, if he will make his home a
positive influence in his life.

We, in Scouting, have laid special emphasis on

the family. The Third Scout Law of Helpfulness includes sharing the home duties. We teach Scouts to practice the Scout Oath and Law in their homes just as much as in Troop Meeting or in camp. Even in our outdoor program we have made provision for sharing activities with parents, and the Scout family hike, Parents' Nights, and Father and Scout dinners are well-known features. We encourage fathers to serve on Troop Committees, as Scoutmasters, Cubmasters, and in other positions of leadership.

Some boys seem to think of their home merely as a place to eat and sleep. They seek their good times outside. They do not share the home duties. Your parents make sacrifices to give you education, pleasures, and other advantages. Don't be a slacker in your responsibilities to them. Be a cheerful and cooperative citizen in your home. Be willing and eager to help the other members of the family. Be glad to make the little necessary sacrifices of your own comfort or inclination for others. Share your interests and your amusements with your parents and learn to take an interest in theirs. Help your mother, not only in her responsibilities in the house, but by your own attitude toward her. Obey instructions promptly and willingly, even though you do not always understand why they were given. By doing this you will not only make your home a happier place, but you will be happier yourself and you will be preparing yourself for a life of happiness, usefulness, and worth-while service.

In the month of May we observe Mother's Day and all of us should try to do something on that day to show our mother or some one else's mother that we appreciate her care and her devotion. Let us do this not just on one day alone. No boy could make a finer gift to his mother than to do his share to make his home happy. Let us make every day Mother's Day in our homes.

> *To be happy at home is the ultimate result of all ambition, the end to which every enterprise and labor tends, and of which every desire prompts the prosecution.*
> —SAMUEL JOHNSON

REVERENCE

As I write, the Second World War is in progress and the threat of war looms on our own encircling horizon. There is uncertainty, there is insecurity reaching down into the very life of each and every one of us. In days like these that try the souls of men it is good to be reminded that our refuge is in God—to hear Washington say:

Our affairs are brought to an awful crisis, that the hand of Providence, I trust, might be more conspicuous in our deliverance. The many remarkable interpositions of the Divine Government, in the years of our deepest distress and darkness, have been too luminous to suffer me to doubt the happy issue of the present contest.

Listen further to the triumphant faith of the immortal Lincoln, who declares:

If it were not for my belief in an over-ruling Providence, it would be difficult for me, in the midst of such complication of affairs, to keep my reason in its seat. But I am confident that the Almighty has His Plans and will work them out; and whether we see it or not, they will be the wisest and best for us.

So convinced was I, as a result of my own early

A SCOUT IS REVERENT

He is reverent toward God. He is faithful in his religious duties, and respects the convictions of others in matters of custom and religion.

experiences, that religion is an essential part of the training of youth that, when we developed our Scout Oath and Scout Law, I gave special attention to the Twelfth Scout Law so as to be sure that it was a part of the obligation of every boy that comes into Scouting. A group of us were entrusted with the task of studying the English Law and developing something that would meet conditions in America. Our meetings covered a period of four months. On some occasions we were in session every day of the week. One of the things of which we were most deeply convinced was the need for what is covered by the declaration of the Twelfth Scout Law: "A Scout is Reverent. He is reverent towards God. He is faithful in his religious duties, and respects the convictions of others in matters of custom and religion."

Sometimes people associate the idea of religion with a definite sect or creed, but reverence does not depend upon any one particular faith. In Scouting, all creeds unite on the basis of tolerance as expressed in this Twelfth Law. To me this is the basis of the spirit of America itself.

It is my belief, and the belief of many of those who are dealing with the problems and welfare of youth, that what the boys and girls of America need most to-day is character development in its truest and fullest sense—they need a strengthening of the religious influence in their lives. The boys and girls of America can not grow into manhood and womanhood of the kind that gives them moral fiber, moral character, without the help and power of God.

The boy or man who has a truly religious attitude of mind is conscious that, as a member of an organized society, he has responsibilities. History and other literature in America have, perhaps, overemphasized the fact that America is the land of the free. America is to-day, as always, the land of opportunity, but not opportunity without obligation. American citizenship as conceived by the founders of our country makes necessary a constant vigilance on the part of all of us, especially in view of the present-day conditions, to develop and keep that reverent attitude of mind that will regard citizenship as a responsibility and not a privilege alone.

Reverence toward God gives the basis for a boy's development, so that he is equipped with a power within himself to know what is right and the motives for doing it; equipped within himself with a power of self-control, so that he can do the thing that is right because his judgment tells him it is right, and refrain from doing the thing that is wrong, because it is wrong. If every boy who reads this message will try to put this Twelfth Scout Law into practice in his daily life, he will soon develop right habits of conduct, moral fiber, character, and self-control, and add to his equipment for a happy as well as a useful and worth-while life of service and satisfaction.

How wonderful it would be if every American, yes, if people the world over would accept and follow the Twelfth Scout Law which so well epitomizes the American Way—the way of Washington, the way of Lincoln, the way of all the immortal multitude of patriots who held fast to faith in God as the sheet-anchor of our liberties.

> *So near is grandeur to our dust:*
> *So near is God to man*
> *When duty whispers, lo thou must,*
> *The youth replies, I can.*
>
> —EMERSON

COURTESY

THE cave-man was all right in his day. He squatted
before the fire, snatched his lump of meat, pulled it
apart with his hands and teeth. If he saw anything
he wanted, he grabbed it. If some one was in his
way, he knocked him down. If the person remon-
strated, the cave-man snarled at him. Often there
was a fight.

But who wants a cave-man around to-day? Along
with houses, tables and chairs, and knives and forks,
we have developed standards of kindness and gen-
tleness and courtesy.

In order to have friends, you must learn to be one.
Perhaps you have sometimes envied those popular
fellows whom everybody seems to like. And yet they
are not endowed with some mysterious power. It is
my belief, based on my experience, that it is within
the power of practically every boy to develop his
ability to attract people and win friendship by being
courteous.

There is no greater asset that any boy can have
than courtesy. I say this on the basis of my own
experience with thousands of boys in all sorts of

situations. Intelligence, skill, perseverance, all these will help you on the road to success. But if your manners are boorish, if you offend people by your rudeness, you are bound to find the going very rough and hard. Other people judge your character by your manners. The boy who knows how to act politely gets the advantage.

Yet courtesy is something that every boy can readily acquire. Some boys do not because they think it is sissified! The really big men in the world have always been noted for politeness and courtesy. Haven't you seen rival captains on the athletic field shake hands with each other? That is courtesy. Theodore Roosevelt was noted for his politeness, especially to the poor and unfortunate. Gene Tunney is one of the most courteous gentlemen I have ever known. Winston Churchill is outstanding in his good manners. History is full of such examples.

What I have in mind is the instinctive kindness to the other fellow that springs from the heart. Don't think that courtesy is something on the outside that you can put on and take off as you do your hat. Real courtesy is based on character. It involves self-control, the ability to check an angry word or a hasty action because you don't want to hurt some one else's feelings. It involves tolerance, the realization that the other fellow has a right to his own convictions and should be allowed to further them.

If you keep these two things in mind, you will never interrupt in an argument, and never start bawling at the top of your voice in a dispute at a ball game. Remember it is the weak man who blusters and shouts because he knows his own weakness of body or mind or character. You won't find that the great men, the fine boys need to do this. They have too much confidence in their own strength and manliness.

I have said that courtesy is one of the easiest qualities for a boy to develop, as well as the most valuable. Will you start now, to-day, and practice for one week, genuine, unfailing courtesy based on good will toward others? If you will honestly undertake to do this, I guarantee that the results will be so pleasing to you that you will decide to keep it up day by day. Courtesy is a habit that can be developed —by you and you alone. Begin to practice in your own home. Try it out on your younger brothers and sisters. Instead of "bawling them out" just try showing them a little courtesy based on kindness.

If you have the sincere wish, you can easily master the simple rules of polite conduct that make life pleasanter and easier for all of us. Observe the manners of other people whose conduct you admire. In most libraries there is a reference book in which you can look up any questions that puzzle you. Do not overlook the importance of knowing the correct thing to do in certain situations. If you begin early, such knowledge will become second nature to you; if you do not acquire it while you are young, you may be embarrassed later in life by the lack of it.

But always remember that real courtesy goes deeper than good manners and surface politeness. Real courtesy involves thinking out opportunities for kindness and service. It is not a matter of form but of the heart. It is the basis of our Scout Good Turn.

Manners are of more importance than laws. Upon them, in a great measure, the laws depend. They give their whole form and color to our lives.

—BURKE

AIM HIGH!

I LIKE to tell young men what Ralph Waldo Emerson, some three quarters of a century ago, said: "Hitch Your Wagon to a Star!" It is just as true to-day, my friends. With a worth-while goal, hard work, training, and the determination to succeed, there is hardly anything that a young man to-day may not hope to attain.

You hear a great deal of discouraging talk to youth these days, and I would not try to minimize that you are growing up in an age of economic uncertainty, hazards, and unrest, war and a threat to our democratic institutions. But look at the other side of the picture!

I was much impressed by some things that Henry Ford, who started his career in a depression, said in regard to the opportunities for youth. "Greater progress lies ahead in the next fifty years than we've had in the last thousand years," said Mr. Ford. "Young people say there are no opportunities to-day. Why, the world's opportunities are just beginning to break! You fellows are going to reduce prices, raise wages, increase production. That's the task youth has ahead. The time is not distant when there will be more jobs than men to do them and youth will have better jobs than to-day." Mr. Ford believes in all sincerity that America does provide a great business opportunity for young people if they maintain their physical strength and health and keep themselves clean in mind and pure in heart.

I am somewhat concerned, I will admit, about what I may term the pauperizing effect of some of the influences on youth to-day. We have so much done for us to make life easier by means of various mechanical appliances that I do think that our young people are deprived of some of the zest of struggle, the deep satisfaction that comes from overcoming obstacles that we had a generation ago. Our young people have not had to pay any price to enjoy the privileges of citizenship in a democracy. They have had to make no effort, bear no struggle. This is not the fault of young people alone but of older people, too. They want others to do what has to be done, turn over to politicians the job of running the community unless there is some very vital local problem affecting them in their homes. Their interest, and even their knowledge about civic affairs is lax.

America needs to be awakened. Our young people need to be awakened. Too many young people to-day tend to sit around waiting for opportunities to open for them instead of getting out and hustling for themselves. If you want to get anywhere you have got to work hard. There is no short cut to success. Find out first what appears to be the shortest way to reach your goal. Remember that what seems to be the quickest way is not always the safest. Then pitch in with all your might.

What you need, as young men starting out on your life's problems, is greater ambition, greater imagination. Approach your handicaps in the spirit of our early pioneers. Our country is still a land of limitless opportunities. Addressing representatives of the Boys Clubs of America, Mr. David Sarnoff, President of the Radio Corporation of America, said that "to enter the race on the road to new achievements, boys need strong heads, strong hearts, strong hands, a firm purpose and clear eyes that are fixed on the objective." To this I would add one thing more—a Goal! Aim high. Don't be satisfied with anything mediocre. The world lies before you. Pick your goal.

> *The actual fact is that in this day opportunity not only knocks at your door but is playing an anvil chorus on every man's door, and then lays for the owner around the corner with a club. The world is in sore need of men who can do things.*
> —ELBERT HUBBARD

"WHAT IT TAKES"

ONE hot July day a Scout named Jimmy reported for duty. An epidemic of septic sore throat was raging in the little town where he lived. Many people had died. Nearly a thousand were ill; the hospital was taxed to capacity and doctors and nurses had been sent in from out of town. Boy Scouts abandoned their plans for camp and volunteered their services to help at the hospital.

One of the doctors sent for Jimmy. The doctor's satchel, containing instruments necessary for an operation early that evening, had been left at a farmhouse several miles up in the hills. Would the Scout see that it was on hand by the required time? The doctor expected Jimmy to use one of the automobiles that was available for emergency service; but Jimmy, under the inspiration of his Scout Promise, saw the request as a personal responsibility and it never occurred to him to involve any one but himself. He arranged for his relief to take over, and trudged up the road.

It is a very different thing to hike through the cool, shady woods with the inspiration of camp and a group of boys with you, from taking a fourteen-mile hike over long, dusty roads, under the blazing July sun, carrying a heavy satchel.

Half an hour before the time for the operation a worried doctor saw an exhausted Scout lugging the bag up the stairs. The doctor realized what had happened, and to make amends, offered Jimmy a dollar bill suggesting that he get a good meal at the restaurant, since it was long after the dinner hour. Jimmy straightened up, looking somewhat puzzled, then he said, "No, I can't take that. Why, that's what we're here for!"

A very good answer, that! Because, to put it in common speech, Jimmy had "What it takes," namely, Scout training. What is the difference between a group of Boy Scouts and a group of other boys? Many answers may be given. To me, the three most important are:

A BOY SCOUT HAS KNOWLEDGE

One summer day on a farm in Idaho a boy was raking hay. A heavy team was pulling, when the bolt which held the neck yoke to the tongue broke, letting the tongue drop. The frightened horses started to run. The boy had no chance to jump. The team broke free from the rake and the broken tongue struck the boy's right leg, running in about three inches and cutting the large artery. Disaster

and death for most boys! Other workers ran up,
but were powerless to help because they did not know
what to do. A doctor was miles away, and although
some one started at once to fetch him, it looked as
if the boy would bleed to death before help arrived.

Yes, but this boy was a Scout! With the help of
the other farm workers he used his First Aid knowl-
edge on himself. He instructed one man how to hold
his thumb on the pressure point, because the punc-
ture was so high it was impossible to use a tour-
niquet. The Scout knew where the pressure points
are and how to apply the pressure. By the time the
doctor arrived, the bleeding was practically checked.
This Scout owes his own life to his Scout training.

A BOY SCOUT HAS SKILL

Another story comes to me from Idaho and in-
volves two groups of boys who were swimming. The
first group were not Scouts. After they finished their
swim, they climbed out of the water and went off
to dress. Two Scouts, as they were walking along the
bank of the pool, suddenly saw a body lying on the
bottom. One Scout immediately went into action in
the way he had practiced again and again in his
Troop. He dived, recovered the body, and because
of his training, was able to bring it to the bank. The
other Scout summoned the rest of the Patrol, who
helped get the body on shore. They gave artificial

respiration while some one went for a doctor, working in shifts as they had been taught, till the boy began to breathe. By the time the doctor arrived he was safe. A few more minutes delay, the doctor said, a little clumsiness, or lack of skill, would have caused a tragedy.

A BOY SCOUT HAS CHARACTER

This story also concerns a rural section of Idaho. It is about a fifteen-months-old baby who fell into an irrigation ditch and was forced through a culvert nearly fifty feet long, to be pulled out unconscious. "He is dead!" cried his parents, and indeed the baby was apparently lifeless. But a Scout was near, an Explorer Scout, and he at once began to work on the motionless little body. "What's the use of going on—the baby's dead!" they said, but the Scout persisted. "Sometimes they've been revived after more than an hour," he replied, as he continued his exhausting work.

Here is where Scout training scored. Older people urged the boy to stop. He was exhausted—he had apparently made no progress—the baby was cold and lifeless under his patient manipulation. No encouragement, no help. Nothing, but grim determination to continue in spite of his aching muscles and exhausted condition. On and on.

And at last the child breathed! Miraculously, this

baby given up for dead by his parents, breathed, cried, and stretched out his arms!

In telling this story, the Scout gave credit to his Scoutmaster who, he said, had taught the Scout all that he knew of First Aid. I give credit to the Scoutmaster and to something that he had helped to develop in the boy—character. Yes, character, that carries on in spite of discouragement and apparent defeat.

Boy Scouts all over the country, because of the knowledge and skill that they have acquired and because of their character are organizing Emergency Service Training Corps, specifically to enable them to be of service to the community in time of any emergency. These are composed of older Scouts, specifically trained in certain skills and possessing equipment that will enable them to coöperate effectively with other agencies should disaster such as tornado, hurricane, or flood take place.

Men are four:
He who knows not and knows not he knows not,
*   he is a fool—shun him;*
He who knows not and knows he knows not,
*   he is simple—teach him;*
He who knows and knows not he knows,
*   he is asleep—wake him;*
He who knows and knows he knows,
*   he is wise—follow him!*
                              —LADY BURTON

HAPPINESS

HAPPINESS is within the reach of practically every boy, no matter what his condition. It can be cultivated and practiced. It does not depend upon money, or position, or pleasure, as some boys—and older people, too—suppose. But it does not come by sitting down and waiting for it. You must get out and find it for yourself. Every day can be filled with happiness, if you will look for it. The best things in the world cost nothing. Physical fitness, for instance, for most of us, depends largely on our own efforts. Good temper, friendliness, courtesy, are assets any boy can cultivate until they become daily habits.

There is a thrill in every worth-while job well done. Here we see the difference between destructive mischief and constructive fun. Some foolish boys try to get a thrill out of causing embarrassment, inflicting pain, reading trashy books, or destroying property. Others get their thrill from a clean game played in the spirit of good sport, from a camp-fire in the woods, from a difficult school lesson mastered. Mischief destroys. Worth-while fun builds up.

Your work is as interesting as you make it. Don't

WHERE ADVENTURE CALLS

The Boy Scout trail to happiness and the greatest of all adventures.

look at it as a handicap. Enjoy it right now. Carry on with all your might. If you attack a job in this spirit, you will be happy in it. The unhappiest boys I know are the lazy ones, the "do-nothing" youths. They accomplish nothing worth while, and are always gloomy about something.

Of course, there will be difficulties. Meet them bravely and cheerfully. Some people think cheerfulness is something easy, that smiles come to certain people without any effort. But often cheerfulness comes only from courage, patience, and determination definitely cultivated.

Another thing that helps make happiness is a variety of interests. The intelligent person with many interests is rarely bored and has a much better chance to achieve happiness. Bored people are dull, and dull people are never happy.

Cultivate appreciation. Learn to enjoy the beauty of nature, a fine piece of team-play in a football game, or some one else's good leadership, or worthwhile record. If one is selfish or conceited he can not appreciate what others do, and he shuts the door to happiness for himself.

Moreover, it is not always the one who has outstanding ability who achieves most happiness or success. Often a man or a boy of quite average capacity is able to accomplish more worth-while things than some one who has brilliant endowments, because of qualities of character which he has, by patient effort, developed in himself. A very important thing, for example, is the ability to get along with people. The earlier in life a boy learns how to coöperate with others, in work and in play, the better his chances are for a happy future.

A joyful home helps bring happiness, but you must do your part to make the home happy and not just accept it as a matter of course. Give this a trial test.

A smile is another thing that helps to bring happiness not only to yourself but other people. A smile based on sympathy and good will helps you and helps all whom you meet.

This brings us to what I believe to be the greatest source of happiness—helping other people. If you want happiness for yourself, you must give equal measure to others. It is giving, not getting that counts.

If it were possible for me to give to every reader of this book gifts that I believe would most surely bring worth-while happiness, I would give something that money can not purchase.

I would give you health—a realization that a strong body is the basis for achievement, and that it is within your own power in practically every case to make and keep yourself physically fit.

I would give you joy in the outdoors and a zest for life in the open—camping, hiking, swimming.

I would give you skill in your life work, and education so that you may make the most of it.

I would give you hobbies, for fun and achievement.

I would give you friendship and the gift of being friendly.

I would give you self-control so that you can do the thing that is right because your judgment tells you it is right, and refrain from doing what is wrong because you know it is wrong.

I would give you the joy of service—service to your home, to your friends, to the community, and to others less fortunate than yourself.

I would give you reverence, recognition of God as Creator and Ruler of the Universe and grateful acknowledgment of His favors and blessing.

> *Happiness consists in activity: such is the constitution of our nature; it is a running stream, and not a stagnant pool.*
> —JOHN M. GOOD

(3)